C000163862

A. M. D.

RULE

OF

THE THIRD ORDER

OF

THE SERVANTS OF MARY.

LONDON:

W. AUSTIN, PRINTER, COLLEGE STREET, CHELSEA.

1 8 8 5.

NIHIL OBSTAT.

Jacobus J. Guiron,

Censor Deputatus.

IMPRIMATUR.

HENRICUS EDWARDUS,

Cardinalis Archiepiscopus.

Westmonasterii,

Die 23 Augusti, 1885.

A. M. D.

FR. PETER FRANCIS MARY TESTA,

PRIOR GENERAL

OF THE ORDER OF

THE SERVANTS OF MARY.

To our beloved Brothers and Sisters of
the Third Order, - health in our Lord
Jesus Christ.

IN OUR most ardent desire of constantly
diffusing, to the greater glory of God,
veneration and devotion to the Sorrows of our
Lady, who is the special Foundress and Patroness of our Order, we have not forgotten
you, beloved Brothers and Sisters in Christ.

Therefore, we earnestly besought the benignity of our Holy Father Leo XIII. to modify somewhat the rigour of the Rule of our Third Order, and to grant unto it more abundant indulgences and favours. The Holy Father received our supplications with his usual benevolence, and by this little book we make known to you his Concessions, in order to satisfy more fully your piety and devotion.

Accept with gratitude the favours of his Holiness, and use them with diligence and profit to the advantage of your Souls and for the prosperity of our Holy Order, which we earnestly recommend to your prayers.

ORIGIN OF THE THIRD ORDER OF THE SERVANTS OF MARY,

AND THE

CLASSES INTO WHICH IT IS DIVIDED.

THERE can be no doubt that, in shedding His most precious Blood for all men, our Divine Redeemer intended every one to arrive first at the light of truth, and then at the light of glory, which He has prepared for those who love Him. And, as in creating man He foresaw, and in His wisdom approved the variety of conditions, which were to follow the increase of mankind; so, in restoring His own work, by Redemption, He did not remove the inequality of various states in society, but rather, He sanctified and consecrated them, furnishing them with a special grace adapted and proportioned to every state. Wherefore, besides making them complete and perfect by

the revelations of sublime mysteries to be
professed by faith, and with moral precepts to
be practised in life, He multiplied them, adding incentives to heroism, and proposing to
His chosen ones the counsels to be followed
in order to reach the summit of perfection.
Hence, the institution of Religious Orders in
the Church. This is not the place to enu-
merate the wonderful fruits brought forth
by these Institutions; but we will mention
those reaped in the middle ages by St. Dominic, by St. Francis, and by our Seven Blessed Founders. The first, by the devotion to
the holy Rosary, crushed the Albigenses; the
second, by embracing the poverty of the Cross
conquered the vanity that corrupts good morals; and the last, being called by the Blessed
Virgin herself to propagate devotion to her
Sorrows, raised a powerful opposition to the
efforts of schism and vice, by which the im-
pious Frederick attempted to lay waste the

mystical Vineyard of Christ. In the designs
of Divine Providence these Heroes of the
Church were but the foundation stones of the
edifice which the mercy of God intended to
raise in His Church for the Salvation of souls.
They were but the first warriors in a battle
which was to be fought by all those who in
course of centuries were destined to undertake
the defence of the Faith. History, which at
the present day by an obvious contradiction is
idolised, as the only source of knowledge, and
is prostituted to prejudice and party spirit, bears
an irresistible testimony to the numberless mul-
titude of men and women, who courageously
gave up the world to meditate under the stan-
dards raised by those champions, that they might
first conquer themselves and then destroy the
forces of Satan. Many who were moved by
the bright example of the heroic virtue of these
followers of Christ, longed to be called the
companions and children of those generous men

who had stretched out their hands to draw them from the mire of vice, and from the confusion of factions. But the austerity of their life frightened the weak, and social consideraations prevented even the courageous from following them. Hence, it seemed as if the work of these holy Founders were still incomplete, since it left many, nay the greater part of men, still exposed to the assault of passions, and in proximate danger of falling back into the abyss, from which, by God's mercy, they had been rescued.

By their Institutions these holy men provided means and helps to avoid the snares and to overcome the enemy. But, either through sloth in some, or through weakness in others, or perhaps on account of the solitude, in which the battle had been fought, these means were often inefficacious to obtain the end. It was necessary, therefore, that the means, which were already powerful in themselves, should be made stronger and that the efforts should be stimulated in order to avoid failure, and to obtain victory. The great Patriarch, St. Francis saw this, and by a Divine inspiration instituted his Third Order, in which the single and the married, the noble and the plebeian, the learned and the ignorant might be admitted; and by dictating holy laws, offered to all a means of defence, and a tie to unite them together without their leaving the secular life in which they were engaged. By the Third Order, St. Francis meant to call back the Faithful to the way of Christian perfection, which was then, as it is now, either neglected altogether, or looked upon as fit only for those who were called to follow the Evangelical Counsels, although Our Lord commanded every one to be perfect, when He said : *"Be ye perfect as your Heavenly Father is perfect."* Now, as the perfection of Christian life consists, essentially, in the perfection of charity, (which is at the same time the seed and fruit of the full observance of the Divine precepts) by his Third Order St. Francis intended to lead men to the obedience of the law of God and of the Church, and to the fulfilment of the duties of their state. And this was most wisely devised; for in this we have the foundation of every degree of perfection, and the abridgement of that to which all men are called.

After the wonderful success obtained by the "little poor man of Assisi," other Founders were induced to imitate his example, and so it happily came to pass, that every Order had its own Tertiaries. Hence it is, that our Seven Blessed Founders first, and then St. Philip Benizi instituted numerous Sodalities of our Third Order in Italy, in France, in Germany, and in other parts of Europe, where persons of every state and condition desired to be admitted. As the Third Order of St. Francis has the glory of numbering St. Elizabeth of Hungary among its members; as that of St. Dominic can boast of St. Catherine of Siena; so our Third Order of the Servants of Mary is blessed by having given to the Church a bright star of holiness in St. Juliana Falconieri. Not only did she make our Third Order illustrious by her virtues and miracles, but also with fervent zeal she propagated it among the noble ladies of Florence and other parts of Italy, calling them together to religious discipline and to a conventual life. To her is due the glory of having given a rule of the higher life to the Sister-Tertiaries, by founding various Communities of the "Mantellate." And while this name, which was then extended to all Tertiaries, was abandoned by other Orders, it was continued, and is still kept in ours; and through the example of that glorious Heroine, many other Convents were established which brought forth abundant fruits of sanctity. Our Third Order

numbers among its members Blessed James,
called "The Almsgiver"; Blessed Johanna
Soderini, the intimate disciple of St. Juliana;
Blessed Elizabeth Picenardi; and many others
recorded in the annals of our Order, amongst
whom special notice should be made of Blessed
Margherita Pecci of Siena, a distant relative
of the reigning Supreme Pontiff. Encouraged
by this great success, and in order to establish
more firmly the good work so wonderfully propagated throughout Europe, under the protection of Our Lady of Sorrows, our Fathers decided to petition the Holy See to approve and
confirm the Rules, which till then had been
observed by the Children of the Third Order
of the Servants of Mary; and Martin V., of
sacred memory, approved and confirmed the
same Rules, ordering them to be scrupulously
kept by all who wished to belong to the
Third Order. The duties contained in this
Rule, the abstinences and fastings, we shall

see later on, when we shall give a faithful translation from the Latin text. But here we may observe that, as to the abstinences and fastings, our Holy Father Leo XIII , in deference to the weakness of the human constitution which is now prevalent, has considerably modified the ancient Rule by two Rescripts, which will be printed after the Rule of Martin V.

Some were of opinion that the Tertiaries of both sexes could not be really so called, or could not enjoy the benefits, indulgences, and privileges of the Order to which they belonged, unless they had made the vow of perpetual chastity. This is not the case ; for, though it be certain that those who have not made the vow of chastity, do not enjoy the privilege of exemption from the jurisdiction of the Ordinary ; nevertheless, by the omission of such vow, they do not cease to be real Tertiaries and to enjoy, thereby, all the benefits attached to the Third

Order, provided they possess all other requisites, which we shall explain further on. To understand this point well, we must observe that there are several Classes of Tertiaries, which, for brevity's sake, may be reduced to four.

FIRST CLASS.

This Class is composed of those Tertiaries who live in community, take the three solemn vows, and profess obedience to Prelates canonically elected. It is evident that these are really Religious, and such is the name given to them by several of the Popes. Like all other Regulars, they enjoy exemption from Episcopal jurisdiction, the privileges and exemptions of Ecclesiastical Law, and many other privileges confirmed and renewed by Clement VIII. in the Bull "*Ratio Pastoralis Officii.*"

SECOND CLASS.

In this Class all Tertiaries are to be enumerated, who though they have taken no solemn vows, bind themselves (but not under sin) to keep the Rule of Tertiaries, live in the Monasteries of the First Order, and wear the religious habit, though not in its completeness. Among the Franciscans, the Tertiaries wear no hood; with us, they have no cloak. Though these are not Religious in a proper sense, because they do not profess the essential vows of the Religious state, and though they are not strictly ecclesiastical persons, nevertheless, by concession of Leo X. in his Bull "*Dum intra mentis arcana*," (which afterwards was confirmed by Clement VIII. in the before-mentioned Constitution) they share the privileges of the Regulars with whom they live. The same may be said of the Tertiaries who live and serve in the Convents of Nuns, provided that such Convents are entirely subject to Regular Superiors. Otherwise, those Tertiaries cannot enjoy the privileges which are not even enjoyed by the Nuns with whom they live, as is stated in the Bull of Nicholas V. "*Etsi cunctorum.*"

THIRD CLASS.

In the Third Class are included those Women who have taken the vow of chastity, either in the unmarried state, or in their widowhood, and who live alone in their houses, or with their relations and kindred, and have property. There is no doubt that these are not Religious, because they have not taken the three essential vows; but still they are on an equality with them, and enjoy all the privileges, exemptions, and indulgences of the Third Order into which they have been admitted. Therefore they may choose their grave wherever they please; they are free from the jurisdiction of the Ordinary; and on account of this exemption they cannot be summoned before any judge, except of the Order to which they belong. In Catholic countries, according to Canon law, they are also free from the civil power, and they share the privileges of the Canon, "*Si quis suadente,*" which subjects to excommunication those who offer violence to them, because they are considered as ecclesiastical persons, having consecrated themselves to God by taking the simple vow of chastity and by resolving to keep the Rule of the Third Order approved by the Holy See, under the obedience and correction of the Regular Superiors, or of their Delegates, from whom they have received the habit.

These Women-Tertiaries may also be admitted to the Divine Offices in the Churches of the Order, during the time of " Interdict "; provided they have not been the cause of it, or have co-operated in it by favour, counsel, or help, or by maintaining it. They cannot however, choose a confessor, except among those approved by the Ordinary, neither can they fulfil the Easter Precept out of their own Parish, as is evident from the Bull of Nicholas IV. "*Supra montem,*" and of Leo X. "*Dum intra,"* and also from the Decrees of the Sacred Congregations of the Council, of Bishops and Regulars and of the Ecclesiastical Immunity. Moreover, the Women-Tertiaries enjoy not only the privileges of personal, but also of local exemption; so that their houses, oratories, churches and chapels (if they possess any) are exempt from the jurisdiction of the Ordinary and of the Parish Priest, nor can they renounce this privilege except by permission of the Roman Pontiff, or with the consent of the General Chapter of the Order. And should these Tertiaries erect, with the consent of their Bishop, (without which the erection would be irregular) a. church, oratory, or chapel on condition of being under the jurisdiction of the Bishop and of the Parish Priest, such edifice (even in this case) would be exempt from the jurisdiction of both, because such a condition is contrary to the privileges granted to the Order, and consequently is to be considered as null

and void. The Bishop or Parish Priest, or any
other, pretending to exercise such jurisdiction
would be liable to the penalties against the
violators of the Privileges of Regulars, as is
laid down by Sistus IV. in his Bulls "*Regi-*
mini" and "*Sacri Prædicatorum et Minorum*
Ordines," which afterwards were abridged by
Leo X. in his Bull "*Exponi nobis fecerunt*
dilecti filii," and were confirmed by Pius V.
in the Bull "*Etsi Mendicantium.*"

Here, however, it must be clearly understood
that, in order to enjoy these privileges, such
Tertiaries have not only to profess the Rule
of the Third Order, to make the aforesaid vow
of chastity, and to live at their own expense in
the house of near relations; but, all this must
appear from a decree of their own Ordinary,
or of the Ordinary of the place in which they
are domiciled; and they must also be subject
to the obedience, correction, and visitation of
the Superior of the Order. It must also be re-

marked that the said Tertiaries living in private houses can wear neither veil, nor wimple, nor scapular; and the Bishop may force them to leave off such articles of dress, even by ecclesiastical censures, as it was decided by the Congregation of Bishops and Regulars, December 20th, 1616. And should these Tertiaries unite together in a Congregation and live like Nuns, they would forfeit their privilege of exemption from the Ordinary, but they would still share the indulgences and spiritual benefits of the Order. The reason of this is, because to enjoy these privileges and exemptions it is required of Women living in community to make the three solemn vows of the Religious state, and to observe perpetual enclosure, as appears from the Bulls of S. Pius V. *"Cura Pastoralis,"* of Gregory XIII. *"De sacris Virginibus,"* and from the Constitution of Clement XII. *"Romanus Pontifex,"* by which he renewed the Bull *"Cura Pastoralis"* of S. Pius V.

FOURTH CLASS.

The Fourth Class of Tertiaries is composed of those Men and Women. married or single, who live in their own houses, and without making the vow of chastity, keep the Rule of the Third Order with submission to the Superior thereof. These do not share in the above-named privileges, as we learn from the Bull "*Dum inter*," of Leo X., and from the decrees of many Congregations. Hence, they are subject to the jurisdiction of the Ordinary and of the Parish Priest, to the Civil Tribunal, and to all the burdens laid on seculars; neither do they enjoy the privilege of the "Canon." But they share, however, the indulgences granted to the Third Order to which they belong, and have the power of choosing their place of burial, and during the time of Interdict they may be admitted into the Churches of the Order to assist at the Divine Offices, provided they have not caused the Interdict, or

co-operated with it in the above-mentioned
ways. Besides, if they are bound to recite the
Canonical Hours, they may use the Calendar
and the Breviary of the Order, as granted by
Paul V. in the Bull " *Ad fructus uberes.*"

But here we must bear in mind that, though
Tertiaries are subject to Episcopal jurisdiction
as to the Sacraments and other ecclesiastical
rights, nevertheless, in everything that con-
cerns the Third Order, they are subject to the
direction and rule of the Regular Prelates.
Hence, by them only can they be deprived of
the Habit and be excluded from the number
of Tertiaries; not because the Regular Prelates
have any jurisdiction over them, but because
they take special care of the Tertiaries' spiritual welfare, being members of the same Order.

Like the Confraternities, these Tertiaries
have their own Superiors, by whom they can
be called together and corrected. Among the
Franciscans these Superiors are called " Min-

isters"; among the Dominicans they are called "Masters" or "Directors," "Priors" or "Sub-Priors," as prescribed by Nicholas V. in the Bull "*Supra montem.*" With us, by the Bull of Martin V., they take the name of "Corrector," " Sub-Corrector," or "Vicar" for Men Tertiaries, and of Prioress for Women Tertiaries. Such Superiors are to be elected by the Tertiaries themselves, or by the Regular Superiors with the advice of the Brother-Tertiaries as to the Correctors, and with that of the Sister-Tertiaries as to the Prioresses. At one time, the respective Superiors of Tertiaries had the power of admitting the Brothers and Sisters to the Habit and Profession. This is no longer allowed; but the express permission of the General of the Order, or of his Vicar, is absolutely necessary, and the Bishop's license is no longer required, as may be shown from the decrees of the Supreme Pontiffs, Innocent IV., Eugenius IV., Martin V., and others

quoted by Legana in the Summa, chap. xiv.,
num. 8.

We have thought it advisable to make these
remarks about the Tertiaries before giving
the Rule of our Third Order, that the reader
may have a clear knowledge of the object
which our Holy Founders had in view in its institution; of the privileges granted to it by the
munificence of the Roman Pontiffs; and of the
various ways of belonging to it. It is evident,
from what we have said that no condition or
state is excluded from the Third Order; and
of all times and ages, the present one, perhaps,
has the greatest need to form holy Sodalities
in opposition to the spirit of wickedness which
is abroad. No arguments are required to con-
vince us of this truth. That same evidence
that shows the triumph of irreligion, shows
also the necessity of uniting together under
the standard of some holy Leader in order to

reform our lives, and to raise, as it were, a living wall for the defence of God's House.

And can we find a better or more succesful Leader than Mary? Like a victorious general She disperses the hordes of hell, conquers heresy, and crushes the head of the Serpent. She is the Mother of fair love, of holy humility, of chaste thought. She chose from the midst of the world seven of the noblest citizens of Florence. She placed them, as seven stars, in the firmament of God's Church, that, by the constant memory of her Sorrows, they might enlighten their brethren to know and love that God who created them, to embrace the Cross of that God who redeemed them, and to meditate on the infinite goodness of that God who, by his charity, sanctified them. At the foot of the Cross, like the Altar of incense before the Ark of expiation and peace, Mary consummated that most sorrowful, though bloodless, sacrifice, which, after the Sacrifice of the Blood of her Son, has not, and cannot have, any other like it. She was also the constant companion of Jesus in the war He waged against sin. Who can doubt, then, her special and powerful assistance to those who under her leadership, and with the same weapons, *viz.*—the memory of, and compassion for her Sorrows—strive to fight bravely against their own passions and against the enemies of God?

If this be so, who can fail to bless the happy day and hour in which he could say, " I am a Servant of Mary, therefore I fight with her to gain a victory over our common enemies"? Who can delay any longer to be enrolled in her holy Sodality, to meditate on her bitter Sorrows, and thereby to conquer and to die bravely fighting as a soldier of Christ? No pen can describe the happiness of him who serves Our Lady, and being clad with the Habit of her Sorrows, becomes Mary's own. In all truth and sincerity he can say : " If Mary is my Leader and my Guide, whom need I fear? If Mary is fighting with me how can I tremble? *'If armies in camp should stand together against me, my heart shall not fear.'* "—Ps. xxvi., 3.

RULE
OF THE THIRD ORDER OF THE SERVANTS OF MARY.

MARTIN, BISHOP,
SERVANT OF THE SERVANTS OF GOD,
IN PERPETUAL MEMORY.

THE wise providence of the Apostolic See benignly favours those persons who, under Regular observance, strive constantly after a devout life, and by its Apostolic power authorises the Rules that are made for their salutary direction, that they may be kept in purity. Now, a petition presented to us by our beloved Sons, the Prior-General and Brethren, and by our beloved Daughters in Christ, the Sisters of the Order of the Servants of Mary, (who live according to the Rule of St. Augustine, and in short are called Brothers or Sisters of the Servants of Mary), has declared that, down to the present time, they have kept and do keep a certain Rule or form of Religious life in which are evidently contained good and reasonable statutes and dispositions adapted to Religious discipline; and though the said Brothers and Sisters of the said Order have received from the Apostolic See various privileges, still, they wish that this Rule, or form of life, may be approved by the same See, in order that their existence may be more sure, and by the aid of Divine clemency, growing from virtue to virtue, they may thus offer to Our Lord a more faithful service. Wherefore the Prior-General and the said Brothers and Sisters have humbly petitioned, that with Apostolic benignity, we would deign to confirm the same Rules or form of life by Our Apostolic power.

We, then, who have received a complete and faithful information of all and each one of these things, being favourable to these petitions, and being pleased and satisfied with the Rule, or form of life, which is clearly and distinctly given in these present papers, word for word, in all its Chapters, and with the aforesaid Statutes and prescriptions, by Apostolic authority and with sure knowledge, confirm and corroborate them by the protection of the present Document; and we will and command that this same Rule, or form of life, be inviolably and constantly kept by the present and future Brothers and Sisters.

The Text of such Rule, or form of life, follows, and is this:

CHAPTER I.

OF POSTULANTS.

First of all, that this Order may constantly advance in holiness of life, which, evidently, depends from admitting well-disposed persons, we will and command that no one be received into this Brotherhood, without the permission of the General of the Order, or of his Vicar,

or of the Corrector assigned for the time being
and for that special place ; nor without a previous examination to prove the good conduct
and reputation of the Postulant, his immunity
from any suspicion of heresy, and his ardent
zeal for the Truth and the Catholic Faith. Fur-
thermore, before taking the Habit of the Order
the Postulant must restore the goods of others,
if he has any in his possession ; he must be
reconciled with his enemies ; and with the
advice and direction of a discreet Confessor,
he must prepare or write his will. Let the same
examination be made for the Women who wish
to join the Order ; moreover, those who are
married cannot be allowed to join the said Sodality without the permission and consent of
their husbands. The same is to be said of married Men, unless there be for them, or for some
of them, a legitimate cause of exemption according to the judgment of the Brothers-Discreet. *

* Discreet, are Officers chosen among the oldest and best
members of the Order.

CHAPTER II.

THE HABIT OF BROTHERS AND SISTERS.

Let all the Brothers and Sisters of the said
Confraternity wear black cloth, which both in
colour and value, must show no signs of
luxury, as becomes the decorum of the Servants of Christ and of the Blessed Virgin
Mary. The tunics, with the sleeves down to
the hand, must be rather narrow and closed
in front; and the belt must be of leather only,
even for the Sisters. Every sort of vanity
must be avoided about their dress, their shoes,
and all their apparel. The veils and the wim-
ples of the Sisters must be of linen or hemp.

CHAPTER III.

BLESSING OF THE HABIT AND RECEPTION INTO THE THIRD ORDER.

The Candidate will be received in the
Chapter-room of the Confraternity or before
the Altar of the Church of the Order, by the

General, his Vicar, or the Corrector of the said Order of the Servants of Mary; and the said General, or Vicar, or Corrector, with the Postulant who humbly desires to be received kneeling before him, in the presence of certain other. Religious of the same Order and certain Discreet from the Confraternity, shall first bless the habit of him who is to be received, according to the form prescribed in the Ceremonial of the Order. The Candidate being thus clothed shall answer "Amen," and be sprinkled with Holy Water by the Prior, Vicar or Corrector; whereupon all the Brothers present shall admit him to the Kiss of Peace. Women are received before the Altar in the same way as we have ordered for the reception of the Brothers.

CHAPTER IV.

FORM OF PROFESSION.

After one year of probation, or even before

if the Novice be considered fit by the General, or Vicar, or Corrector, or by the one deputed, and also by the greater part of the Professed of the Sodality, let him be admitted to the Profession according to *the Ceremonial of the Order.* Women also will make this profession in the same way before the General, or, as aforesaid, and also in presence of the Prioress, or of some other deputed by her.

CHAPTER V.

THE DUTY OF PERSEVERANCE IN THE ORDER.

We decree also that none of the Brothers or Sisters of this Sodality or Order may leave it and return to the world after having made their profession; but they can pass to an approved Order where the three solemn vows are made.

CHAPTER VI.

THE RECITATION OF THE CANONICAL HOURS AND OTHER VOCAL PRAYERS.

The Brothers and Sisters will say the Canonical Hours daily, if not prevented by illness. For Matins they will say twenty-eight *Paternosters*, for Vespers fourteen, and seven for each of the other Hours; and at each of the Hours they shall say the same number of *Ave Marias*, in honour of the Ever-Blessed Virgin Mary. Before meals let them say one *Paternoster*, and after meals the same, or the Psalm *Miserere mei Deus*, or the *Laudate*, if they know them. Likewise the Symbol of the Apostles, viz: *Credo in Deum*, is to be said, by those who know it, before Matins and Prime, and after Compline. But those who know and recite the Canonical Hours, (*e. g.* Ecclesiastics,) are not bound to say the above-mentioned *Paters* and *Aves*.

CHAPTER VII.

The Time to Recite the Hours.

All shall rise for Matins on Sundays and
Feasts of Obligation, from the Feast of All
Saints to Easter. But during Advent and
Lent they will rise in the night. Those,
however, who are occupied in manual labour
may recite in the morning the Hours even to
Vespers exclusively, and in the evening they
will say Vespers and Compline together.

CHAPTER VIII.

Confession and Communion.

Four times a year at least, that is at Christmas, Easter, Pentecost, and the Assumption
(or Nativity) of the Blessed Virgin, all shall
diligently confess their sins, and endeavour
to receive with fervour the Sacrament of Holy
Eucharist, unless some one for just reasons
is prevented by his Confessor. And if any

one wishes to receive Holy Communion oftener during the year, he will do so with the permission of his Superior and the blessing of God.

CHAPTER IX.

Keeping Silence in the Church.

While Mass is being said and the Divine Office sung, or God's word preached in the Church, silence must be diligently kept by all, and attention paid to prayer and to the divine office; and if by necessity something is to be said, it must be spoken in a low voice.

CHAPTER X.

Reverence due to the Prelates of the Church.

Let the Brothers and Sisters visit with devotion their Parish Churches, according to the direction of the Canons and laudable usages; and let them show great respect to their Bishops and the other Prelates of the Church.

▲

Their rights must also be fully satisfied as to the tithes and other customary obligations.

CHAPTER XI.
FASTS.

Both Brothers and Sisters shall fast every day from the first Sunday of Advent to Christmas, and from Ash-Wednesday to Easter-Sunday, every Friday in the year, and on all Fast-days commanded by the Church. If any one wishes to observe extra Fasts or make other austerities, he will ask permission from the Superior or take the counsel of a prudent Confessor.

CHAPTER XII.
USE OF MEAT.

The Brothers and Sisters may use meat on Sundays, Tuesdays, and Thursdays. On all other days they will abstain, unless they are ill, or weak, or travelling, or if one of the principal Feasts falls on that day.

CHAPTER XIII.

Going-out, Balls and Banquets.

Let the Tertiaries avoid wandering about the town from curiosity. The Sisters, especially the young ones, should not go out alone; and all Tertiaries should avoid weddings, balls, worldly banquets, theatres, or such like vain amusements. And no one can undertake a journey, even a pious pilgrimage, without a special license from the General, his Vicar, or the Father Corrector.

CHAPTER XIV.

Carrying Weapons.

The Brothers shall not carry weapons, not even in self-defence, except to fight for Holy Faith, or for other reasonable causes, and with the permission of their Prelates.

CHAPTER XV.

Visit and Care of the Sick.

The Father Corrector will appoint two

Brothers who, on hearing of the illness of a Brother, will endeavour in charity to visit him as socn as possible. From the beginning they will induce him to make his confession and to receive the other Sacraments of the Church; and, if circumstances require it, they will give him temporal assistance so far as they conveniently can. But if the sick person be poor, let them procure what is necessary for him, either of their own, or of what they may have in common, according to their means. The Sisters will do the same when one of the Sisters falls ill.

CHAPTER XVI.

DEATH AND SUFFRAGES OF THE BROTHERS AND SISTERS.

The death of a Brother shall be communicated to the other Brothers of the same town or place, that they may be present at the funeral rites and burial. The same is to be done by the Sisters, when one of them dies. Within eight days of the burial of the dead, each Priest-Brother will say Mass for the Soul of the Departed; the Brothers and Sisters who can read the will say a Psalter (fifty Psalms); and the others will say one hundred *Paternosters* and *Requiem æternam*. In the course of the year everyone will have three Masses said for the Brothers and Sisters living and dead; those who can read will recite the whole Psalter, and the others will say fifty *Paternosters*.

CHAPTER XVII.

ELECTION OF THE CORRECTOR AND OF THE PRIORESS.

When the Corrector dies or is removed, the Prior, or his Vicar, with the counsel of the elder members of the Third Order, will elect another Corrector. Every year, within the Octave of Easter, the said Prior, or his Vicar, will consult, in a private meeting, the elder

members as to the removal or confirmation of
the Corrector, and will remove or confirm him
as he, with the Council, deems it to be expedient. In like manner, the Father Corrector,
with the advice of the said Prior, or his Vicar,
and of the same elder members, may decide
about the Sub-Corrector, or Vicar, and may
confirm or remove him as they may deem it
to be more expedient. The Sub-Corrector, or
Vicar, has no more authority than the Corrector may give him. The same is to be done
in regard to the election and removal of the
Prioress.

CHAPTER XVIII.

Duties of the Corrector and of the Prioress.

The Correctors will observe all that is prescribed by the Rule and will see that it is kept
diligently by all the other Brothers. If any
one breaks it, or is negligent, he is to be chari-
tably corrected and punished by him; or he

may, if he thinks it more desirable, refer the case to the Prior, or his Vicar, that they may administer the correction. It will be the duty of the Prioress to be most careful to attend the Services of the Church, to exhort the Sisters to the observance of the Rule, to watch with diligence, either by herself or by deputy, the conduct, behaviour, and dress of the Sisters, that nothing in them may scandalize others. She will take a special care that the Sisters, particularly the young ones, do not become too intimate with any man, unless there be a relationship in the third degree at least, and the man is of good morals and behaviour.

CHAPTER XIX.

CORRECTION OF BROTHERS AND SISTERS.

If anyone is noticed to have allowed himself to take undue familiarity, and, after having been warned three times, he has not corrected himself, he shall be excluded for some time

from the Chapter and the society of the Brothers. And if he does not amend himself, let
him, with the advice of the Discreet-Brothers,
be publicly excluded altogether from the Order,
and be not re-admitted till all the Brothers
think him to be reformed. If, likewise, any
one utters injurious words against a Brother
or any other person, or, being in anger, strikes
any one, or ventures to go to a place forbid-
den to him, or shall have in any other way
disobeyed, or have told a wilful lie to his
Superior, let him be punished more or less
severely, according to the condition of the
person and the nature of the fault, either by
fasting on bread and water, or by exclusion
from the Chapter or from the society of the
Brothers. Again, if any one has committed a
sin against the Sixth Commandment let him
(after the counsel of the greater part of the
Professed Brothers of that Branch) be punished
according to the gravity of the fault, and the

condition of the person, but in such a way as
to be an example to the others. And if he
refuses to undergo the assigned penance, let
him, with the advice of the Discreet, be ex
pelled from the Order. As to the correction
of the Sisters, we order the same as for the
Brothers.

CHAPTER XX.

MONTHLY MEETINGS TO BE HELD IN THE
CHURCH OF THE SERVITE FATHERS; AND THE
SUBJECTION OF THE BROTHERS AND SISTERS
TO THE GENERAL AND THE PROVINCIALS OF
THE ORDER.

The Prior, or his Vicar, will call together
all the Brothers once a month in the Church
of the Servite Fathers to hear the Word of
God, and the Holy Mass if the hour permits
it; and on this occasion the Prior, or his Vicar,
will read and explain this Rule, and will tell
the Brothers what is to be done, will correct
and punish those who have been negligent,

as he shall judge expedient in the Lord and according to this Rule. On the first Friday of each month let the Sisters meet together in the said Church to hear the Divine Word and the Holy Mass; the Rule must be read and explained to them also, and their defects corrected as we have said above. We order also, that in each town or village where there are Brothers and Sisters, a suitable Corrector or Vicar be assigned to them, who should be a Priest of the Servite Order, whom they have asked for, or who has been chosen by the Priors and Vicars, either by themselves or through others. Moreover, we order and decree that each and all the Brothers and Sisters of the said Confraternity, in any place whatever, for their better supervision and profit, be entirely subject to the direction and discipline of the said Prior General, or Provincial in all things concerning their mode and manner of life.

CHAPTER XXI.

Dispensation for a Reasonable Cause.

The Corrector of the Third Order, in the case of Brothers, and the Prioress with the Deputed Vicar, in that of Sisters, may dispense with the abstinences, fasts, and other austerities mentioned in the preceding Chapters, when, for some legitimate cause, they think it advisable.

CHAPTER XXII.

Obligation of this Rule and Manner of Life.

Finally, as it is said in the Constitutions of the Order of St. Augustine, so in respect to this Rule, or Manner of Life, we wish every one to hold as certain, that, with the exception of the Divine Commandments and the laws of the Church contained in it, the Brothers and Sisters are not bound by it under sin, but under penalty only, which being imposed by the Superior or by the General, is to be humbly accepted and promptly performed by the transgressor, by the co-operation of the grace of Jesus Christ our Lord and Redeemer, who with the Father and the Holy Ghost liveth and reigneth, true God, for ever.   Amen.

Let no man, therefore, be permitted to annul or contradict with daring boldness, this Document of our confirmation, monition, will, and command.   And if any one shall attempt to do so, let him know that he shall incur the anger of God Almighty, and of the blessed Apostles Peter and Paul.

Given in St. Peter's at Rome on the 16th day of March, in the Seventh Year of our Pontificate.

TWO RESCRIPTS
OF HIS HOLINESS LEO XIII.

I.

MOST HOLY FATHER,

The Father General of the Order of the Servants of Mary, humbly prostrate at the feet of Your Holiness, entreats the three following favours for the Tertiaries of his Order :—

1.—That they may twice a year receive the Papal Benediction, with the Plenary Indulgence attached.

2.—That they may on the Feasts of Christmas, Easter, and Pentecost, as well as on the Feast of the Seven Dolours (celebrated in September), receive from any of their Confessors the Benediction, with the Plenary Indulgence attached.

3.—That the daily recital of the *Our Father*, *Hail Mary*, and *Creed*, prescribed by the Rule, be reduced to the number of fifty-four *Our Fathers* and *Hail Marys*, and three *Creeds*.

4.—That in case, by reason of ill-health, or any other sufficient cause, the Tertiaries are unable to keep the fasts and other abstinences prescribed by their Statutes, their several Confessors shall have authority to commute the said fasts and abstinences into other pious works, as they shall judge fitting.

His Holiness Leo XIII. in the audience granted the 16th day of December, 1882, to the undersigned Secretary of the Holy Congregation of the Indulgences and Sacred Relics, graciously consented to bestow the favours in all particulars as requested. Granting that the present should have effect in perpetuity without the publication of a Bull, all things whatsoever to the contrary notwithstanding.

Rome from the Secretariat of the said Holy Congregation, December 16, 1882.

Louis Card. Oreglia di S. Stefano.
Prefect.

✠

FRANCIS DELLA VOLPE,
Secretary.

II.

MOST HOLY FATHER,

The Prior General of the Servants of Mary, prostrate at the feet of Your Holiness, declares that, in these days of persecution, the Third Order of the Servants of Mary, through the devotion to her Sorrows day by day increasing, is wonderfully gaining ground, not only in Italy, but also outside of Europe. As however, in the Rule approved by Pope Martin V. in the Constitution *Sedis Apostolicæ Providentia,* in cap. VI. XI. and XVI. certain obligations are prescribed, which, either from the conditions of the times, or the circumstances of individuals, are now difficult, or almost impossible of fulfilment, Your Holiness, in order to second the piety of the faithful towards the Queen of Martyrs, is humbly entreated so to reduce them, that they may be easily performed by every class of persons. The obligations spoken of are the following:—

1.—In Cap. VI. *Of Prayer* : the recitation of 77 *Paters*, (already reduced by Your Holiness to 54) is prescribed instead of the Canonical Hours.

2.—In Cap. XI. *Of Fasts* : a fast is prescribed for the whole of Advent, and all Fridays throughout the year, with abstinence from meat on all Mondays and Wednesdays.

3.—In Cap. XVI. *Of Suffrages* : the recitation of 50 Psalms, or 100 *Paters*, with the *Requiem æternam*, for those who cannot read, is prescribed in intercession for every Tertiary deceased, for whom the Priests must celebrate a Mass; in addition, it is prescribed to every Tertiary to have three Masses celebrated in the course of the year, and to recite the whole Psalter, or for those who cannot read 50 *Paters*, for the salvation of the Brothers and Sisters both living and dead.

Then, in regard to the Indulgences for the said Tertiaries, the petitioner humbly declares that up to the present time they have enjoyed no other Indulgences than those proper to the First and Second Order of the Servants of Mary, and that only by way of communication. But, as no document exists proving this privilege of communication, and as on this account room is left for doubt and uncertainty as to the acquisition of the Indulgences, Your Holiness is entreated to deign to concede directly to the Servite Tertiaries these Plenary and Partial Indulgences, as well as such privileges as Your Holiness may think most advisable.

HIS Holiness Pope Leo XIII., in audience granted on December 15th, 1883, to the under-signed Secretary of the Holy Congregation of Indulgences and Sacred Relics, having heard the expression of the opinion in reference to the aforesaid prayer of a Consultor of the said Holy Congregation, graciously consented that the three Articles of the Constitution *Sedis Apostolicæ Providentia* in question, in which Pope Martin V. approves the Rule· for the direction of the members of the Third Order of the Servants of Mary, should be modified in such a way that the present and future members of the said Third Order, instead of the aforesaid obligations should be bound only to the following :

I. Those who do not recite the Canonical Hours, or the Little Office of the Blessed Virgin, shall say, every day, twelve *Our Fathers,* twelve *Hail Marys*, and *Glory be to the Fathers*, provided they be not hindered by illness.

II. They shall fast on the Eves of the Feasts; 1st, of Our Lady of Dolours (in the month of September); 2nd, of the Seven Blessed Founders; 3rd, of St. Juliana Falconieri.

III. They shall all assist at the obsequies of every deceased Brother or Sister, and recite the Rosary of Our Lady's Dolours; the Priests in offering the Sacrifice of the Mass, the Laity in partaking of the Holy Communion shall pray for the repose of the soul of the deceased Brother or Sister. All the Tertiaries shall recite on one day at their discretion, within the the year, the Rosary of the Seven Dolours for the Brothers and Sisters living and dead; every layman shall make three Communions, and every Priest shall offer a Mass for the same intention.

Moreover, the Holy Father, while cc

pletely withdrawing the Indulgences and privileges which the Tertiaries of the Order of the Servants of Mary have hitherto enjoyed, whether by communication from the First and Second Order, or granted under whatsoever circumstances, and under whatsoever title or form, and while withdrawing, abolishing, and abrogating such communication, if it ever existed, has deigned to grant directly to the Tertiaries of the Servants of Mary the Indulgences both Plenary and Partial, and Privileges ennmerated in the following summary.

SUMMARY OF PLENARY INDULGENCES.

1.—Tertiaries of either sex, being truly penitent, having made their confession and communion, may obtain a Plenary Indulgence:
I. On the day of their entry into the Order.
II. On the day of their profession.
III. On the Feasts—1, of Corpus Christi; 2,

of the Immaculate Conception of Our Lady;
3, of the Nativity; 4, of the Anunciation;
5, of the Purification; 6, of the Assumption;
7, of Our Lady of Sorrows; 8, of St. Joseph,
Spouse of the Blessed Virgin (19th March);
9, of St. Peregrine Laziosi; provided that with
the above dispositions they shall devoutly
visit some Church or public Oratory, and pray
for some space of time for the intentions of
the Supreme Pontiff.

IV. Once a year, if for eight days consecu-
tively, they shall attend a Retreat.

V. At the hour of death, if with the aforesaid dispositions, or at least with a contrite
heart, they shall invoke with their lips, or if
they have lost the use of speech, in their
hearts, the Most Holy Name of Jesus.

VI. In like manner, if on the days of the
Stations mentioned in the Roman Missal, they
shall visit their Church, Oratory, or Chapel,
and there pray for the wants of Holy Church.

they shall gain the same Indulgences that they would gain by personally visiting the Churches within or outside of Rome.

VII. Those who shall recite five *Our Fathers*, *Hail Marys*, and *Glory be to the Fathers*, for the wants of Holy Church, and one *Our Father, etc.*, for the intentions of the Supreme Pontiff, may gain once a month, the Indulgences of the Stations of Rome, of the Portiuncula, of the Holy Places of Jerusalem, and of St. James of Compostella.

VIII. Twice a year on receiving the Papal Benediction, if they pray for the intentions of the Supreme Pontiff; and likewise on the same condition those who shall receive the Benediction on the following days—1, of the Nativity of Our Lord Jesus Christ; 2, of the Resurrection; 3, of Pentecost; 4, of Our Lady of Sorrows (in the month of September); 5, of the Seven Blessed Founders; 6, of St. Philip Benizi; 7, of St. Juliana Falconieri.

Partial Indulgences.

On the day on which the Brothers and Sisters shall assist at the monthly meeting or conference, they may gain the Indulgence of seven years, and seven quarantines.

Privileges.

Masses that shall be celebrated in intercession for the Brothers and Sisters, in whatever Church or Chapel, shall be privileged.

All the aforesaid Indulgences may be offered on behalf of the holy souls in Purgatory.

The present Decree shall last in perpetuity without the publication of any Bull, anything whatsoever to the contrary notwithstanding.

Given in Rome from the Secretariat of the above Sacred Congregation, the 15th of December, 1883.

Louis Card. Oreglia di S. Stefano,
Prefect.

✠

Francis Della Volpe,
Secretary.

DECLARATIONS & EXPLANATIONS
ON.
THE VARIOUS ARTICLES OF THE RULE OF THE THIRD ORDER.

THE Third Order, in the intention of the glorious Patriarch St. Francis, was to conduce to the perfection proper to every state of life, rendering participators in the advantages of the Religious Life, those who, desiring with true goodwill to serve God, could not abandon their families nor turn their back on the world, in order to seclude themselves in the Cloister. That which the Seraphic Patriarch intended, was also the design of other Founders, in increasing the religious families founded by them respectively, by the addition of the Third Order in imitation of St. Francis. With this object, they framed a Rule for them, afterwards approved by the

Roman Pontiffs, commanding its observance
by those who desired to join the Third Order.
That of our Third Order of the Servites was
approved and enjoined by His Holiness Martin V., and it is the one which we have above
described. But, since it appears in some points
to be somewhat obscure, we think it well to
add here some declarations and explanations.

Having said this, it is necessary, in order
to interpret it rightly, to call to mind what
we have noted, in speaking of the origin and
nature of the Third Order. We said, therefore,
that there were four classes of Tertiaries.

To the first belong, those who profess the
three solemn vows, and live in community
under the rule of Regular Prelates; as well
as the Sister Tertiaries, who having professed
the vows, live perpetually enclosed. Of the
second are those who, without solemn vows,
live in community with the First or Second
Order. To the third class belong those Si-

Tertiaries, who having taken the vow of perpetual chastity, live on their own means with near relations in the first or second degree of consanguinity or affinity. In the fourth are classed those who live in their own homes without vows, either married or single.

Now the Rule, speaking of the Tertiaries in general, embraces all these classes indiscriminately, and therefore, in regard to those who live in community, it may and should be rigorously applied; due exceptions being made for those who live in the world, or in the midst of their own families. Because for these, owing to their circumstances, some obligations must be regarded as difficult, or impossible of execution. Hence, it is for this reason that we deem it opportune to give some explanation of the various heads of the Rule, that they may not be to any one a cause of scruple or trouble of conscience.

CHAPTER I.

Aspirants to the Order.

Under this head are enumerated the qualities the Postulant must possess in order to be admitted to the Third Order, which are, to be of virtuous life, of good reputation, free from all taint of heresy, and on the contrary, zealous for the Catholic Faith. Three conditions must be fulfilled before a Postulant can be admitted or receive the habit; they are—1, that if in possession of another man's property, it must be restored; 2, that he must make his will; and 3, that if married, the consent of the husband, or wife, must be given in a formal document.

In regard to the first condition, it is necessary to remark, that by "another man's property" is commonly understood property acquired furtively, or by bad faith, not property borrowed at interest, or as a loan, gratuitous or other-wise, as some writers have erroneously interpreted. Whosoever, therefore, desires to enter the Third Order, must first restore, if he have such, ill-gotten goods. In regard then to debts, legally contracted according to necessity and various contingencies, it suffices that justice be done by satisfying them according to arrangement with the creditors. Certainly in regard to Tertiaries who, withdrawn from the world, and live in community, they should be held subject to the regulations which the Holy See has laid down for aspirants on entering the First Order, one of which is, that they be not burdened with debts. Tertiaries, on the contrary, who remain in the world in the midst of their families, may be in such circumstances as to be obliged to contract debts. Such debts then can be no hindrance to admittance and profession in the Third Order.

Concerning the second condition, which refers to the making of the will before being admitted into the Order, it may be fitting to remark that, although this is in some way necessary for Tertiaries living in their own houses (since in cases of sudden death where no will is to be found, contentions, even serious, often arise), yet this condition is binding more especially on those who live in community, and who ought thus to disengage themselves from all worldly thoughts and cares. In fact we read of the Ven. Sister Diana Davanzati that, before being admitted into community-life with the Tertiary Sisters, she made a full renunciation of all her goods by means of a document legally attested by the public Votary.

In regard then to the third condition, that in the case of married people, the wife must have the consent of her husband, and the husband that of his wife: it is well to observe that as Tertiaries, both men and women, are bound to observe a certain moderation and modesty in dress, to attend certain exercises of piety and devotion, and keep established fasts and abstinences; it is well and prudent that married people, before being admitted to the Order, should have such consent from their partners in order not to incur disputes and quarrels, to avoid which they would be under the necessity of transgressing the Rule. It is not, however, necessary that such consent should be made in attested form, save where they desire to separate by mutual consent, in order to live in community.

CHAPTER II.

HABIT OF THE BROTHERS AND SISTERS.

What is said under this head of the quality and make of the Habit applies only to the Tertiaries, both men and women, who live in community. In fact whilst veil, bands, etc., are spoken of here, a Decree of the Holy Congregation of Bishops and Regulars, published

on December 16th, 1616, absolutely forbids
Sister-Tertiaries living in their own houses
to wear the veil, the wimple, and the hood.
Tertiaries then, living in the world (except
those who take the vow of perpetual chastity)
may wear the dress of the make and quality
usual in the place of their residence, and suitable to their condition in life. They should,
however, take care to observe Christian modesty, and avoid, as much as is in their power,
all that may savour of ostentation, pomp, and
vanity; since it is becoming in the Servants of
Mary to show, even outwardly in their dress,
that holy humility which is the foundation of
Christian perfection. Under their ordinary
dress they will wear the little hood and the
leather girdle. At the Meetings, both ordinary and extraordinary, and on all occasions
when they do not care to wear the complete
habit, they should at least endeavour to assist
in a black dress; and after death they should

be dressed and buried in the complete Tertiary habit.

The Sister Tertiaries, then, who take the vow of perpetual chastity, though in the fashion of their dress they may follow common usage, will always wear black in memory of the widowhood of Our Lady of Sorrows.

CHAPTER III & IV.

BLESSING OF THE HABIT; AND THE MANNER OF RECEPTION INTO THE THIRD ORDER.

On the occasion of clothing a Sister, the Corrector shall be assisted by the Sisters, and specially by the Prioress, or Vicaress, and by the Mistress, or Second Mistress of Novices; and, in like manner, in the clothing of a Brother, he shall be assisted by other Brothers. The same applies to the profession.

Let it be observed, that when the Brothers and Sisters assume the habit, or are professed, if they have confessed and communicated they may gain the Plenary Indulgence granted by our Holy Father Leo XIII., in the Rescript of December 15th, 1883.

CHAPTER V.

OBLIGATION OF 'PERSEVERING IN THE ORDER.

This Chapter applies exclusively to the Tertiary Brothers and Sisters who live in community, under simple and solemn vows. In reference to Brother Tertiaries who live in their own houses, here is what has been written on the matter by our learned and pious Father Arcangelo Giani: "At the present day, when there is not the usage of living together, it does not appear that this Chapter need give rise to any scruple; though indeed a wise and prudent counsel may be drawn from it to endeavour to persevere in this Holy Confraternity, advancing always in good, and

B

not to harbour the capricious idea of abandoning such a work, by which progress on the road to Heaven is so much facilitated."

CHAPTER VI.

RECITAL OF THE CANONICAL HOURS AND OF OTHER VOCAL PRAYERS.

Since the Tertiary must be distinguished from the ordinary Secular, and emulate the Religious, he is bound to imitate the latter in his principal office, which is praising God. This is the office of Angels, and very dear to holy souls. The saintly Prophet David, amid the many and onerous cares of his kingdom, never omitted to praise God seven times a day, and an ancient legend of the glorious Foundress of the "Mantellate," St. Juliana Falconieri, says that she usually devoted ten hours of the day to prayer, often twenty, and sometimes passed the entire day in prayer and

and ecstasies of love, without partaking of food of any sort.

The Holy See, in rendering the Tertiaries sharers in spiritual advantages and privileges not granted to the ordinary Faithful, wishes them to more especially distinguish themselves in exercises of piety. Indeed, under this head, it prescribes that in prayer they shall imitate the Religious of the same Order, reciting, like them, the Canonical Hours, which consist, (for those who do not recite either the Divine Office or the Little Office of Our Lady), in the repetition of 77 *Our Fathers* and *Hail Marys*, divided as said above in Cap. VI., *Of Prayer.* Our Holy Father, Leo XIII., however, now happily reigning, considering the difficulty of fulfilling a somewhat burdensome obligation, consented to the request of the Most Reverend, the Father General of the Order, and by the Rescript of December 15th, 1883, (given at the end of the Rule), reduced the fulfilment of this obligation for those Tertiaries who do not recite the Divine Office or that of the Blessed Virgin, to the daily repetition of twelve *Our Fathers*, *Hail Marys*, and *Glory be to the Fathers*.

CHAPTER VII.

Time of Reciting the Hours.

From the annals of the Order we learn that when Pope Martin V. promulgated the Bull in which he approved the present Rule, the Sister Tertiaries who lived in Community without enclosure, constituted almost a separate Order. They assembled in Chapter and elected the Provincial Superioresses and the Superioress General, who, however, depended upon the Superior of the Order, without whose consent they could not remove the Sisters from one house to another; and they went in a body to the Church of the Order at the time of divine worship. Now, however, as the Tertiaries do not live in community, and as it is not the usage to recite Matins at night, what is here prescribed is not binding. Here is what is said on the subject, by the above-quoted Father Giani : " Which observance (that of getting up at night for Matins) must have been much easier in those times when the Sisters lived together, than at the present day, when it may be much more excusable, if it be not completely observed; hence, there need be no ground for scruple on the part of those who do not observe this good practice, submitting themselves always to the advice and guidance of the Father Corrector." The same may be said of men Tertiaries, for though it might be less inconvenient for them to go out alone to Church by night, still as it is no longer the usage to recite Matins by night, the obligation under this head ceases also with respect to them.

CHAPTER VIII.

CONFESSION AND COMMUNION.

The Yearly Communions prescribed by the Rule are four, the same number which in the time of Martin V. were prescribed for all the faithful. At present, by the tenor of the Rescript above granted, which is appended to the Rule, there are ordered by the Holy Father Leo XIII. a Confession and Communion for the soul of every Brother and Sister deceased, and three times a year for all the Brethren and Sisters living and dead. Notwithstanding this, it does not mean that then and afterwards the Tertiaries approached the Holy Sacraments so rarely; since we read of St. Juliana Falconieri, " that she passed several days of the week without taking any other food than the Holy Communion," and likewise of the Blessed Elizabeth Vieri, of Siena, " that she communicated very frequently." The Venerable Sister Eleonora, also of Siena, three times a week fortified herself with the Bread of Angels; and so with many other holy souls who illumined our Order by their virtues.

Hence, the Superiors General of the Order have always inculcated on their Tertiaries frequent reception of the Holy Sacraments of Confession and Communion. And it will be an excellent practice to frequent them especially on the following Feasts, so as to gain also the many Indulgences granted on such solemnities by the Roman Pontiffs. The Feasts are:—Christmas, the Circumcision of Our Lord, the Epiphany, Holy Thursday, Easter, Ascension Day, Trinity Sunday, Corpus Christi, the principal Feasts of Our Lady, those of the Saints and Blessed of the Order, as well as of the Holy Apostles, Peter and Paul, of St. Joseph, St. Anne, St. John the Evangelist, and the first and third Sunday of every month. Any who desire to approach the Holy Table more frequently, can do so with the advice of a discreet and prudent Director, to whom the decision of such a delicate matter ought to be referred.

CHAPTER X.

REVERENCE TO BE SHOWN TO THE PRELATES OF THE CHURCH.

Ordinary Tertiaries not being exempt from the jurisdiction of the Bishop, it follows that they must regard him as their Superior, and show him all those acts of respect and obedience which are suitable to his dignity and condition. The same may be said of the Parish Priest under whose jurisdiction they live, and from whom they must receive the Easter Communion, and the holy Sacraments at the hour of death. Indeed, they should remember that in both of the duties named they should give an edifying example to all the Faithful.

CHAPTERS XI. & XII.
Fasts, and the use of Meat.

In the history of our Third Order, we find
examples of most severe fasts and penances.
Thus, St. Juliana Falconieri, as has already
been mentioned in the note to Chapter VIII.,
passed several days of the week without taking
any other nourishment than the Holy Communion. Of the Venerable Anna Juliana Gonzaga,
Archduchess of Austria, it is recorded that
she fasted on bread and water every Friday,
as well as on the Vigils of the principal Feasts
of Our Lady, and twice a week used the discipline on herself severely. Of the Venerable
Sister Angela Maria Cavallotti, it is narrated
that she fasted three days of the week on
bread and water; and of the Blessed Margaret
De Sanctis, that she never drank wine or ate
meat or milk food, but that her daily nourishment consisted solely of herbs and vegetables.
Notwithstanding this, having regard to the

weakness of modern constitutions, and for
other reasons easy to be understood, the Holy
Father Leo XIII., in the above-mentioned
Rescript of the Holy Congregation of Indulgences, of December 15th, 1883, moderated
these two clauses on fasts and abstinences,
dispensing altogether from the latter, and prescribing that the Tertiaries, over and above
the fasts prescribed to all the Faithful, shall
observe as a fast, only the Vigil of Our Lady of
Dolours in September, (that is, the Saturday
before the third Sunday of that month); the
Vigil of the Seven Blessed Founders of the
Order of the Servants of Mary (10th February)
and that of St. Juliana Falconieri (18th June).
If then any Tertiary, Brother or Sister, with
the permission of his Spiritual Director, should
wish to observe any other fast, or any abstinence, or should wish to conform to the Rule,
he will always perform an act most acceptable
to God, and most beneficial to the soul, since

our Venerable Father Anthony of Siena used
to say, that abstinence is a most powerful
bulwark to defend the virtue of the soul.

CHAPTER XIII.

GOING-OUT, BALLS, AND DINNERS.

Taking part in the pomps, vanities, and
gaieties of the world is ill-befitting such persons as have the blessing to belong to an
Order whose distinctive work is humility and
mortification, since it was instituted for medi-
tating on the sorrows and humiliations suffered
by the Most Holy Virgin in this world, and
in order to propagate devotion to them.
Therefore, in intercourse and conversation with
others, either at home or abroad, the Tertiary
Brothers and Sisters should seek to show in
all their actions, that moderation, prudence,
gravity, and modesty suitable to those who
profess a special service of Our Lady of

Dolours, giving to others a good example, and a stimulus to virtue.

On the other hand, considering the conditions of the times, and the customs widely introduced even into good Christian families, the observance of this Chapter may prove extremely burdensome, or at least very difficult to a large number of Tertiaries. If, however, all cannot strictly observe the letter, they may at least try to adhere to the spirit of the Rule. While the custom, too, has become prevalent, of absenting themselves without asking permission of the Corrector, it would yet be well to give him notice, though it were only to justify their absence from the meetings. Theatres then, places of public entertainment, public balls, and noisy weddings, are prohibited by this Section; and exception is only to be made for those who, being dependent on the will of another (as are the children of a family and married women), could not abstain from them without incurring serious inconvenience. What is said of these public amusements, sinful in most cases, if not in all, is not intended to apply, and should not be extended to the so-called family amusements, which are held at certain times among relations, friends, and acquaintances. In these, provided Christian modesty be duly observed, all excessive and unbecoming dissipation be avoided, and there be no danger of scandal, Tertiaries of either sex may take part, such amusements not being included in the prohibition of the present Chapter.

CHAPTER XV.

VISITING AND ATTENDING THE SICK.

One of the works of mercy is to visit and attend the sick. How acceptable this work is to God, we learn from the mouth of Our Divine Redeemer Himself, who speaking of the general judgment (St. Matthew, chap. 2⁵

v. 36), says that He will call His elect to participate in His eternal glory, enumerating the meritorious works they performed, and will say to them, "*I was sick and thou didst visit me.*" *Infirmus (eram) et visitastis me.*

If, however, as Christians we are bound to practise works of mercy towards our neighbour, the order of charity requires that for this exercise we should always prefer such persons as are bound to us by the nearest and most binding ties, and with whom we have consequently the most intimate relationship. Membership of the same Order is a spiritual bond so close as to unite us all in true brotherhood. And in the same manner as consanguinity renders brothers in blood equals and sharers in the same manner, in all the temporal goods of the family, so this spiritual relationship by a perfect, because spiritual tie, renders each a sharer in the spiritual goods of the other. Being then all spiritual brothers in Christ, we must mutually assist each other in all necessities, and especially in case of illness. It is then rightly prescribed that the Brothers and Sisters infirmarians, immediately on receiving intelligence of the serious illness of any members of the Order, shall visit them frequently, administering spiritual aid to them in the form of good advice and exhortation, preparing them when necessary for the worthy reception of the Holy Sacraments, and giving timely notice to the Corrector, that he may impart to them the Absolution *in articulo mortis*, to which is attached a Plenary Indulgence. In addition to spiritual comforts, they should try to administer to them such temporal aids as may be necessary and opportune, imitating the example of the holy Foundress of the Order of the *Mantellate*, who used to go to the hospital to assist and console the sick, often restoring them to bodily health by the touch of her blessed hands, not shrinking from a^r

proaching her pure and saintly lips to kiss and
suck their wounds and sores; in the highest
degree glad and joyful, when she could make
her meals on the remnants of their food sup-
plied to them by charity. Our Venerable
Victor of Cremona used to say, that greater
merit is acquired in a single day's attendance
on the sick, than in a whole year of fasting.

CHAPTER XVI.

Prayers for the Dead.

Charity unites us here below as members
of one body and of one household, for which
reason we call each other by the sweet names
of Brothers and Sisters. As, however, charity
is principally directed to our spiritual welfare,
it ought not to cease by the termination of
the bodily life, that is to say, we must not
restrict ourselves to loving our Brothers and
Sisters as long as they live amongst us, but

our love must be extended to those who have
completed their earthly pilgrimage and been
called by God to their eternal home. They,
who have passed away, perchance with debts
to the Divine Justice still undischarged, have
to atone in Purgatory for faults committed
here, before they can be admitted to participate in the joy of the Saints. There those
holy souls suffer, without being able to merit
any mitigation of these pains, which though
transitory, are yet most severe. Our charity
alone by prayers and intercession can lessen
them, and even shorten their duration. Hence,
the Holy Church, a most tender Mother of her
children, exhorts us to intercession for the departed, and opens to them the treasure of her
holy Indulgences. In the Second Book of the
Macchabees, the piety of Judas Macchabeus
is praised for this, that at the close of a battle
against Gorgias, he made a collection, and
sent the money obtained to Jerusalem, that a

Sacrifice might be offered in propitiation for the soldiers slain in battle; and it is said, that it is a holy and salutary thought to pray for the dead.

Hence, the Holy See in this Chapter, when speaking of the death of the Brothers and Sisters of our Confraternity, prescribes what is to be done on such occasions, and the prayers to be recited in propitiation for them, which however, being somewhat lengthy and imposing an obligation not easy of fulfilment for all, our Holy Father Leo XIII., in the above-quoted Rescript of the 15th December, 1888, reduced them; prescribing—1st, that all the Brothers and Sisters shall assist at the obsequies of the Brothers and Sisters deceased, (for which purpose the relations are exhorted, immediately after the death to notify it to the Father Corrector, informing him of the day of the funeral, in order that he may then announce it to the Brothers and Sisters);

2nd, They shall recite for the departed a Rosary of the Seven Dolours; 3rd, The Brothers who are Priests, shall recommend the departed soul to God in the Holy Sacrifice of the Mass, and the Lay Brothers and Sisters shall receive a Communion in intercession for the departed; 4th, Within the year also the Lay Brothers and Sisters shall recite a Rosary of Our Lady of Sorrows, and make three Communions, and the Priests shall celebrate a Mass for the members of the Order, living and dead.

CHAPTER XVII.
Of the Election of the Corrector and the Prioress.

In this Section it is ruled that the Corrector shall be elected by the Prior, or Vicar, with the advice of the Elders of the Confraternity. Usage, however, now prescribes that, in places where the First Order exists, the Corrector shall be elected by the Most Reverend, the

Father General, or by the Prior. But, in regard
to remote places, where there are no Religious
of the Order, and where the Most Reverend
Father General is unacquainted with the candidates, and therefore cannot himself make the
choice, the Corrector must be proposed to him
by the Brothers themselves, or by the Sisters.
In Mexico and in Spain, where our Third
Order flourishes, the custom is to propose
three individuals, of whom the General, or his
Vicar, selects one. Hence arises the necessity that there should be in the Third Order
a Council composed of Brothers or Sisters,
commonly termed the 'Discreet,' who in case of
the death or removal of the Corrector, assemble
and elect the Priest whom they deem worthy
and capable of filling the office, and present
him to the General, or his Vicar. Be it noted,
however, that the said Priest shall be a member of the Third Order, or at least, shall be
desirous to enter it and be professed.

It is also the office of the Discreet, to meet on receiving notice from the Corrector, in order to treat of the affairs which concern the interests of the Confraternity, as also to elect such as seek admittance into it. In a word, they form the Council over which the Corrector presides. In addition to the Discreet, in the case of the Sisters, the following Officers shall be elected, *viz :* the Prioress (to whom will appertain the right of selecting her own Vicaress), the Secretary, the Mistress and Second Mistress of Novices, the Treasurer, and the Infirmarians. These Officers will also form part of the Council of the Discreet.

CHAPTER XIX.

OF THE CORRECTION OF THE BROTHERS OR SISTERS.

It will also be the duty of the Corrector, should any member of the Confraternity prove incorrigible, to assemble the Council of the Discreet, and after reporting his serious failings, and. trying proper means of correction, and after having previously obtained the consent of the Most Reverend, the Father General, to decide on his expulsion from the Confraternity.

CHAPTER XXI.

OF DISPENSATIONS WHICH MAY BE OBTAINED FOR REASONABLE CAUSES.

In this Section, when authority is conferred on the Prioress to dispense the Sisters on legitimate grounds, from abstinences, fasts, and other austerities, it is the Tertiaries living in community that are spoken of. In regard to those living in their own homes, in addition to the Corrector, their own Confessors also have authority to commute these obligations in consideration of the peculiar necessities or circumstances of each, as the reigning Pontiff has given permission by the Rescript of the Holy Congregation of Indulgences, given on 16th December, 1882.

MAXIMS,

Dictated by St. Philip Benizi to St. Juliana Falconieri for the direction of her Sisters, which may also serve as a rule of life for the Tertiaries of the Servants of Mary :

The Tertiary Sisters ought ever to bear in mind, that they are placed in this world in order themselves to combat, and to be opposed by others.

They should regard the Most Holy Virgin not only as the purest of virgins, but also as the most humble and obedient of spouses.

In order to imitate the Mother of Sorrows, they should esteem the sorrows above the joys of life, since it is impossible to combine the joys of the world with the service of God.

They should despise the vanities of worldly dress in order worthily to wear that of the Order; and not only refrain from exceeding therein their proper condition in life, but even should profess holy humility in externals, as befits the true Servants of the Blessed Virgin.

They should attend to their families, and the management of the same, with that charity which makes all things succeed and prosper, and without that over anxiety which produces distraction of mind.

They should combine their devotions with peace and harmony in their families; the service of God in the world being incompatible only with sin, and not clashing in any degree with natural relations and duties.

Let them make no account of the jests and sarcasms directed by worldly people against those who lead a pious and retired life; always remembering the words of the Apostle—'If I were to please men, I should not be a servant of Christ.'

Let them reflect that, if the good they may do be not always praised by men, any ill they might do would certainly be exaggerated beyond that of other women.

Let them seek to be always usefully employed, since an idle heart is easily filled with the vanities of the world.

In affliction, let them have recourse to God and to the sovereign Comfortress of the afflicted, without caring to be consoled by creatures.

Let them undertake nothing without previous and mature deliberation; and let them never regard the maxims of human prudence which do not accord with the Divine Law.

They should fly the esteem of the world, without, under a pretext of devotion, showing contempt for individuals.

They should be equally charitable to all the Sisters, without making invidious distinctions between the poor and the rich.

Let them seek to observe their Rule with fidelity, strengthening themselves with the fervour of devotion and penance to keep it well.

DIRECTORY

OF THE THIRD ORDER OF THE SERVANTS OF MARY.

In order that the Confraternity of the Third Order may increase and flourish to the honour of God and Our Lady of Dolours, and for the spiritual good of souls, it is necessary that its members should be animated by a true spirit of devotion, obedience and concord. Hence, in order that there may be uniformity between the several Congregations existing in various places, and all grounds of dissension among their members may be removed, we will now give some brief directions and rules regarding the functions of the various Offices which are to be performed in them. We will also point out the mode of proceeding for the election of the Officers, leaving other and more minute arrangements to the prudence of individual Correctors and Counsellors. These, taking into consideration the special circumstances of time, place, and person, will be able to take such measures as they may deem to be suitable, asking, when they find it necessary, the advice of the Most Reverend, the Father General of the Order.

THE CORRECTOR.

The Corrector is the representative of the Most Reverend, the Father General of the Order, and hence is the true and faithful head of the Congregation over which he presides.

It is, therefore, his duty to examine the Postulants, who cannot be received or professed without his consent. Consequently, although the Council of the Discreet may for good and sufficient reasons refuse the Postulants proposed by the Corrector, they have no authority to admit those whom he has rejected. It is his place, moreover, to preside over the Council of the Discreet, and at the Monthly Meetings; and in case he be prevented, he will appoint as his representative, either his Vicar, or one of the Discreet in the place of the Brothers; or the Prioress, or another Discreet Sister, if it be a meeting of the Sisterhood. It will likewise be his office to watch over the exact observance of the Rule; to reconcile all differences that may arise between Brother and Brother, between Sister and Sister, or between one Congregation and another; and to give a final decision on all questions that are not referred to the examination and judgment of the Discreet, with whom the sentence would then rest. But in case the difference lay between the Corrector and the Council of the Discreet, the matter would then be referred to the Most Reverend, the Father General, with whom would rest the final sentence, to which all must humbly bow.

THE COUNCIL OF THE DISCREET.

. The Corrector, as President of the Council of the Discreet, the Vicar, the Master of Novices, the Treasurer, the Secretary, the Infirmarian, and the Sacristan, if there be one, are Councillors *ex officio.* In like manner, for the Sisters, the Prioress, Vicaress, Mistress of Novices, Treasurer, Secretary, Infirmarian, and Sacristan, are *ex officio* of the Discreet. The others are elected, as will be stated hereafter, in such number as the Corrector, in the exercise of his discretion, shall deem proportionate to the greater or lesser number of their members. The Council, or Discreet body, shall be always presided over, as has been said above, by the Corrector, or in his absence, by the Vicar. At the Meetings of the Council, when it is summoned by the Corrector, all the members composing it (unless they be reasonably hindered), are bound to be present. Meetings shall always be opened with the recital of the prescribed prayers.

The Discreet Brothers or Sisters in their Meetings will consider the well-being of the Congregation, discussing and inquiring into the means best calculated to promote its increase. They will also discuss any extraordinary outlay which has to be incurred on behalf of the Congregation, and decide on the manner of meeting it. They will decide, also, by secret vote, on the admission of Postulants, and on the expulsion from the Con-

gregation of any members, men or women,
whose conduct may have rendered them un-
worthy to belong to it. Whenever a vacancy
occurs for any office, the election (by secret vote)
of the candidate proposed by the Corrector
will rest with the Council; but the nominee
will keep his post only for the time that must
elapse before the general election of the Officers.
Should any dispute or difference arise in the
Congregation, in case it cannot be arranged
by the Corrector, it may be referred to the
Council. Whenever a question that requires
a secret vote, is under consideration, it shall
always be decided by an absolute majority of
votes. The Discreet Councillors shall remain
in office for the space of one year.

THE VICAR.

The Vicar shall be elected solely by the
Corrector, and shall remain in office until

he be removed by him, or replaced by another. His functions shall be determined by the Corrector himself, on whose absolute discretion will depend their extension or restriction, as he shall deem most expedient for the service of God.

THE PRIORESS.

To the Prioress belongs the first place after the Corrector, both in the Meetings and in the Councils of the Sisters. Her duty will be to watch that the Officers fulfil their duty, and to receive requests for admittance into the Congregation, delegating either the Mistress of Novices or another Sister to make strict inquiry into the circumstances and conduct of the Postulants. She will then refer the requests, with all the particulars, to the Corrector, that in due time he may report them to the Council of the Discreet. She will also watch over the maintainance of harmony between the Sisters; will admonish delinquents with charity and prudence; and in case any Sister, regardless of her admonitions, should be a cause of scandal or of dissension to the others, she will bring the same to the knowledge of the Corrector.

THE VICARESS.

The Vicaress shall be nominated solely by the Prioress, whom she will represent in whatsoever the Prioress herself cannot do. She too will have a voice in the Council of the Discreet.

THE MASTER OF NOVICES.

The Master of Novices shall have a voice in the Council of the Discreet. His office is to give or explain the Rule to such as desire to be admitted into the Third Order; to en-

c

quire into their circumstances and conduct; to accompany to the Altar and assist the Novices in the ceremonies of their reception or profession. During the period of the Novitiate, it will be his duty to inculcate on the new candidate the observance of the Rule and perseverance in the good work undertaken. Above all, he should be exact in the fulfilment of his own duties, in order to give a good example, especially in punctuality in attending the Meetings. The same holds good of the Mistress of Novices in regard to the Sisters.

THE BROTHER OR SISTER SECRETARY.

The Brother or Sister Secretary must keep with accuracy the list of the Brothers or Sisters, both professed and Novices, always registering the Christian and surnames, as well as their names in the Order, those of their parents, their country and residence, and the day of their reception and profession. It will also be their duty to send out notices both for the Monthly Meetings, and for those of the Discreet or Council. On them is laid the duty of drawing up Reports of the matters discussed or decided in the Council. It will also be their duty to have the Reports signed by whomsoever has presided over the Council, and by one of the Discreet, if a Council of the Brothers be in question, or by the Prioress, if it be one of the Sisters. The Brother or Sister Secretary will also, whensoever directed by the Corrector or Prioress, have the charge of sending out notices of the deaths of the Brothers or Sisters respectively, that the usual prayers may be offered for them.

THE BROTHER OR SISTER TREASURER.

The Brother or Sister Treasurer will keep in a place of safety, the alms, money, or articles of value belonging to the Confraternity; and when any heavy or extraordinary outlay arises, shall dispose of them in such manner as the Committee of the Discreet or Council shall determine, and not otherwise. Inconsiderable and slighter expenditure may, however, be authorized by the sole consent of the Corrector or Prioress. Ordinary and necessary expenses, such as those of postage, &c., may be defrayed without asking express permission —authority for payment being implied in the appointment to the Office.

THE BROTHER OR SISTER SACRISTAN.

The functions of the Brother or Sister Sacristan will be to see that the Chapel or Oratory be kept clean and decently adorned, and to prepare everything requisite for the holy Offices, both ordinary and extraordinary.

He will have the care of all the sacred utensils
and fittings belonging to the Confraternity,
and it will fall to his charge to prepare for the
holy Rites, at the close of which he will return
everything to its proper place. He will assist
punctually at all ceremonies, as well as at
receptions and professions. And since he will
have to make purchases, if they are ordinary
and trifling, he may do so, showing the bills
afterwards to the Corrector (or in the case of
a Sister Sacristan, to the Prioress,) who will
then give the order for payment to the Treasurer. Should they be·extroardinary and of
large amount, they cannot be made without
the consent of the Committee of the Discreet
and Council, who may be convened for the
purpose even for an extraordinary sitting.
Otherwise the Brother (or Sister) Treasurer is
not entitled to pay the amount ; and should
he do so, may be condemned by the Council
to bear the expense himself.

THE BROTHER OR SISTER INFIRMARIAN.

Amongst the Officials are also the Brother or Sister Infirmarian, whose charge it will be to visit and assist the sick Brothers or Sisters respectively. It is earnestly recommended to all the Brothers, that whenever one of them falls ill, notice should be given to the Infirmarian, by some one in the house, or by some Brother or Sister of their acquaintance. The Infirmarian, on receipt of such notice, will repair with diligence to visit the invalid, to endeavour to console him. In case the illness be of a serious character, he will repeat his visits more frequently, to comfort him and exhort him to patience and resignation in his sufferings, according to the example of Our Lord in His Passion, and of Our Most Afflicted Mother. In case the illness be not only serious but dangerous, he will inform the Corrector, that he may visit the invalid, and comfort him with salutary advice and admonitions, and may at the fitting time console him with Absolution *in articulo mortis*, by means of which a Plenary Indulgence may be gained. In order that the sick may want no necessary assistance, the Corrector may elect a number proportioned to the need of under Infirmarians, selected with the consent of the Infirmarian, instructed by whom they will fulfil their duties with zeal and charity. All that is said here of the sick Brothers and their Infirmarian, applies also to the sick Sisters and their Infirmarian. On the occurrence of the death of any Brother or Sister it will be the duty of their respective Infirmarians to notify the same to the Corrector, that through the Brother or Sister Secretary, he may order the prescribed prayers of intercession.

———

THE ELECTIONS.

All the Officials, and the Discreet, whether

Brothers or Sisters, will remain in office for a year, after which the Elections will be renewed, according to the following mode of procedure :

A month before the election of the Officials the Corrector will give notice in a Public Meeting, fixing the day, hour and place of its assembling ; and at the same time he will give notice in writing of the said elections to the several Electors.

In the interval, he will seek to confer with them in order to ascertain their feelings in regard to the continuance of the old Officials and Counsellors, or to the election of new ones to fill their places, endeavouring with prudence and charity to reconcile discordant opinions in order to obtain unanimity for the day of the election.

The day fixed for the election having arrived, the Electors will assemble at the hour appointed, each taking with him a sealed paper, with the name and surname of all the Officials whom it is proposed to elect. After having recited the prescribed prayers, each Elector will lay his paper on the table at which are seated the Corrector with the Vicar, or with a Brother not an elector, expressly invited to attend. When all the papers have been handed in, the Corrector will open them one after the other, and read aloud the names of the candidates.

The Vicar, or the Brother Assistant, will register the results with care. All the papers having been opened and read, the number of votes given for each candidate will be examined, and those who have secured a majority will be declared Officials for the coming year. It is a matter of course that no Elector can vote for himself. For the legality of the Election it is necessary that the papers should be signed by the Electors with Christian and surname, in order that, in case of a dispute, the regularity of the Election may be proved.

We say 'in case of dispute,' because the list of signatures must be closed and sealed, so that its contents shall not be seen, and is only to be opened by order of the Corrector with the advice of the discreet members of the Confraternity.

At the close of the Election, the Vicar, or Brother Assistant, will draw up a statement of it and insert the same in the records of the Confraternity, with the signatures attached of the Corrector and the Discreet Brothers only, as well as of whomsoever shall have drawn up the statement as Secretary.

The same course is to be followed in the election of the Officials by the Sisters, with the sole difference that the Corrector shall be assisted by a Sister who is not an Elector, to act as a Secretary, whenever the Vicar shall not be present.

THE ELECTORS SHALL BE —

1. All the Discreet Brothers or Sisters and the Officials in office.

2. All who have in the past filled the places of Discreet Councillors and Officials.

3. Such Brothers or Sisters as the Corrector shall deem worthy to belong to the electorial body.

Within a month after the Election of the Officials, that of the Discreet Brothers or Sisters will be proceeded with, and it will be effected, not by written lists, but by secret votes on the approval of the Corrector, and only those shall be held elected who shall have secured at least one vote more than the full half of those recorded.

The Election of the Discreet rests with the Officials alone, and together with them, will remain one year in office.

These Rules and enactments the Brothers

or Sisters of our Third Order will strive sedulously to observe, so as to merit the Benediction of our Most Afflicted Mother.

METHOD OF
ESTABLISHING A NEW CONGREGATION
OF THE THIRD ORDER

As soon as it comes to pass that in a given place there are a sufficient number of Brothers or Sisters of the Third Order, (authority having first been received from the Most Reverend, the Father General, and a Corrector having been appointed by him), the Corrector will assemble the Brothers or Sisters in the Chapel selected where there shall be an Image of Our Lady of Dolours, before which there shall be lighted not less than four candles, when he, wearing a cotta and stole of the colour of the day, will intone the Hymn Veni, Creator Spiritus, *with the Response and Prayer as at page* 123, *to which will be added the following Prayers:*—

Omnipotens sempiterne Deus, qui misericordia tua hos fideles specialiter aggregasti; in eorum corda, quæsumus, Paraclitum, qui a Te procedit, infunde; illosque in tua fide et caritate corrobora, ut temporali Congregatione proficiant ad æternæ felicitatis augmentum.

Deus qui de vivis et electis lapidibus, æternum majestati tuæ præparas habitaculum; largire his fidelibus benedictionem tuam, ut et ipsi tamquam lapides vivi superædificentur super lapidem vivum, Dominum nostrum Jesum Christum filium tuum.

Interveniat, quæsumus, Domine Jesu Christe nunc et in hora mortis nostræ, apud tuam Clementiam, Beata Virgo Maria Mater tua, cujus sacratissimam animam, in hora tuæ passionis doloris gladius pertransivit. Per Te, Jesu Christe, Salvator mundi, qui cum Patre et Spiritu Sancto vivis et regnas in sæcula sæculorum. Amen.

Then seating himself, he will read the diploma of the Most Reverend, the Father General, conferring powers for the establishment of the Congregation, after having read which he will deliver a brief discourse on the excellence of the Third Order, and on the Privileges and Indulgences granted by the Holy See to the Brothers or Sisters. The discourse being finished, the nomination of the Discreet Councillors and Officials, according to the Rules presented and explained in the Directory, page 103. He will then recite the Hymn Te Deum, which will be sung by all standing:—

HYMN.

Te Deum laudamus : * Te Dominum Confitemur.

Te æternum Patrem : * omnis terra veneratur.

Tibi omnes Angeli : * Tibi cœli et universæ potestates.

Tibi Cherubim et Seraphim : * incessabili voce proclamant.

Sanctus, Sanctus, Sanctus, * Dominus Deus Sabaoth.

Pleni sunt cœli et terra, * majestatis gloriæ Tuæ.

Te gloriosus * Apostolorum chorus.

Te Prophetarum*laudabilis numerus.

Te Martyrum candidatus *laudat exercitus.

Te per orbem terrarum * sancta confitetur Ecclesia.

Patrem * immensæ majestatis.

Venerandum tuum verum,*et unicum Filium.

Sanctum quoque*Paraclitum Spiritum.

Tu Rex gloriæ* Christe.

Tu Patris*sempiternus es Filius.

Tu, ad liberandum suscepturus hominem, * non horruisti Virginis uterum.

Tu, devicto mortis aculeo, * aperuisti credentibus regna cœlorum.

Tu ad dexteram Dei sedes,*in gloria Patris.

Judex crederis*esse venturus.

Te ergo quæsumus, tuis famulis subveni* quos pretioso sanguine redemisti.

Æterna fac cum Sanctis tuis * in gloria numerari.

Salvum fac populum tuum Domine, * et benedic hæreditati tuæ.

Et rege eos, * et extolle illos usque in æternum.

Per singulos dies,*benedicimus Te.

Et laudamus nomen tuum in sæculum, * et in sæculum sæculi.

Dignare, Domine, die isto, * sine peccato nos custodire.

Miserere nostri, Domine, * miserere nostri.

Fiat misericordia tua, Domine, super nos, * quemadmodum speravimus in Te.

In te, Domine, speravi : * non confundar in æternum.

P.—Benedicamus Patrem, et Filium cum Sancto Spiritu.

R.—Laudemus et superexaltemus eum in sæcula.

P.—Confirma hoc Deus, quod operatus es in nobis.

R.—A templo sancto tuo, quod est in Jerusalem.

P.—Memento Congregationis tuæ.

R.—Quam possedisti ab initio.

P.—Domine exaudi orationem meam.

R.—Et clamor meus ad te veniat.

P.—Dominus vobiscum.

R.—Et cum spiritu tuo.

OREMUS.

Deus, cujus misericordiæ non est numerus, et bonitatis infinitus est thesaurus ; piissimæ majestati tuæ pro collatis donis gratias agimus, tuam semper clementiam exorantes ; ut, qui petentibus postulata concedis, eosdem non deserens, ad præmia futura disponas.

Da nobis quæsumus, Domine, perseverantem in tua voluntate famulatum ; ut in diebus

nostris, et merito et numero populus tibi ser-
viens augeatur.

Deus, in cujus Passione secundum Simeonis
Prophetiam, dulcissimam animam gloriosæ
Virginis et Matris Mariæ doloris gladius pertransivit : concede propitius ; ut, qui dolores
ejus venerando recolimus, passionis tuæ effec-
tum felicem consequamur.

Deus, qui ad recolendam memoriam dolorum
Sanctissimæ tuæ Genitricis per Septem Beatos
Patres, nova Servorum ejus familia, Ecclesiam
tuam fœcundasti: concede propitius; ita nos eorum consociari fletibus ut perfruamur et gaudiis.

Deus, qui Beatam Julianam Virginem tuam
extremo morbo laborantem pretioso Filii tui
Corpore mirabiliter recrearo dignatus es :
concede, quæsumus; ut, ejus intercedentibus
meritis, nos quoque eodem in mortis agone
refecti, ac roborati ad cœlestem patriam per-
ducamur. Per eumdem Christum Dominum
nostrum. *R.*—Amen.

In conclusion, he will give the Benediction with the Blessed Sacrament, or if this cannot be done, he will bless those present, saying—

Benedictio Dei omnipotentis, Patris, ✠ et Filii, et Spiritus Sancti descendat super vos et maneat semper.   Amen.

The Corrector will place in the Archives the Register of Admissions and Professions, with the authentic attestation of the Erection of the Congregation written and signed by him in the following terms :—

Anno Domini —— die —— mensis —— Ego, Infrascriptus N. Prior, (*vel* Corrector, *vel* Sacerdos), facultate Rmi P. Magistri —— Prioris Generalis Ordinis Servorum B. M. V. munitus, erexi Congregationem Tertii Ordinis Servorum B. M. V. in loco ——, præsentibus Testibus ——. In quorum fidem cum ipsis Testibus me subscripsi.

MANNER OF CLOTHING THE TERTIARY SISTERS WHO MAKE A VOW OF CHASTITY.

The Altar of the Church or Chapel of the Congregation having been fittingly adorned with the Antipendium of the colour of the day, there shall be placed on it in due order the Garments to be blessed, the Stole likewise of the same colour, the Vessel of Holy Water with the Aspersorium, the Ritual of the Order, and in front of the Altar at the Gospel side, there shall be placed a chair.

The Sisters being assembled in the Chapel at the appointed hour, the Corrector goes to Altar, and taking the stole and putting it on, seats himself. Meantime, the Sister about to be clothed, accompanied by the Mistress of Novices, and by another Sister (if there be not a second Mistress) advances into the middle of the Chapel, and there with her two assistants

kneels down and in a distinct voice repeats the
Confiteor, *at the end of which the Corrector*
stands up, and says:—

Misereatur tui Omnipotens Deus, et dimissis
peccatis tuis, perducat te ad vitam æternam.

R.—Amen.

And then :—

Indulgentiam, absolutionem, et remissionem
peccatorum tuorum tribuat tibi omnipotens,
et misericors Dominus.

R.—Amen.

Then, the Sister about to be clothed still
remaining on her knees, the Corrector turns to
the Altar to bless the clothing, and says aloud,
the assistants replying :—

P.—Ostende nobis, Domine, misericordiam
tuam.

R.—Et salutare tuum da nobis.

P.—Dominus vobiscum.

R.—Et cum spiritu tuo.

Blessing of the Girdle.

Oremus.

Omnipotens, sempiterne Deus, qui pietatis tuæ misericordiam quærentibus, et veniam peccatoribus tribuisti, oramus immensam clementiam tuam, ut hanc Corrigiam bene ✠ dicere, et sancti ✠ ficare digneris, ut quæcumque lumbos suos ad evitandam concupiscentiam ex ea præcincta fuerit continentiam perpetuam, et misericordiam consequatur. Per Christum Dominum nostrum.

R.—Amen.

The Veil.

Oremus.

Quæsumus, omnipotens Deus, ut Velamina ista famulæ tuæ capiti suo imponenda bene ✠ dicere digneris, quatenus in eis ros tuæ benignitatis descendat, et sint hæc Velamina

super caput ipsius honestas, humilitas, et
sanitas cum omni bene ✠ dictione Dei Patris,
Filii, et Spiritus Sancti, per merita Beatissimæ semper Virginis Mariæ.

R.—Amen.

The Tunic, Scapular, and Mantle.
Oremus.

Domine Jesu Christe, qui tegimen nostræ
mortalitatis induere dignatus es, immensam
tuæ largitatis abundantiam obsecramus, ut hoc
genus vestimentorum, quod Sancti Patres
nostri ad innocentiæ, humilitatis, et patientiæ
indicium, Beatissima Virgine id sibi divinitus
suggerente, ferre sanxerunt, ita bene ✠ dicere
digneris, ut hæc famula tua, quæ illis corpore
induta fuerit, mente pariter, ac animo induat
te Jesum Christum Salvatorem nostrum.

R.—Amen.

The Rosary and Book.

Oremus.

Domine Jesu Christe, Fili Dei vivi, qui discipulos tuos orare docuisti, suscipe quæsumus Orationes famulæ tuæ quæ cum tua bene ✠ dictione a te semper incipiant, et per te cœptæ finiantur. Qui vivis, et regnas Deus in sæcula sæculorum.

R.—Amen.

He then sprinkles the Habit and the Sister about to be clothed, repeating the Antiphon, Asperges me. This done, he seats himself again, and in the meantime the Sister, with her two companions, rises, advances and kneels on the highest step of the Altar. The Corrector then, assisted by the Mistress of Novices and the other Sister, divests her of her worldly clothing, saying :—

Exuat te Dominus, carissima Soror, veterem hominem cum actibus suis, ut renoveris spiritu mentis tuæ, et induaris novum hominem, qui secundum Deum creatus est in justitia, et sanctitate, in Christo Jesu Domino nostro.

R.—Amen.

On giving the Tunic.

Accipe, carissima Soror, talarem Tunicam in signum gravitatis, et modestiæ.

R.—Amen.

The Girdle.

Accipe Corrigiam super lumbos tuos, ut sint lumbi præcincti, in signum castitatis, et temperantiæ.

R.—Amen.

The Scapular.

Accipe Habitum munditiæ, et humilitatis, ut ita induta observes ea, quæ regularibus institutis, et majorum præceptis mandantur.

R.—Amen.

THE MANTLE.

Accipe Clamydem nigram in signum pœnitentiæ, et mortificationis, ut, mortua mundo, Deo, ejusque Sanctissimæ Matri perpetuo vivas. R.—Amen.

THE VEIL.

Accipe Velamina candida, cœlesti benedictione respersa, in signum innocentiæ ad operiendam umbratilem capitis, pectorisque tui venustatem, atque ad æterni decoris speciem jucundissimam consequendam.

R.—Amen.

THE ROSARY AND BOOK.

Accipe signum Orationum in manibus tuis, ut more contemplantium, præsentem vitam habeas in patientia, atque futuram gloriam quærens, spreto mundo, cupias dissolvi, et esse cum Christo.

R.—Amen.

And on giving the Lighted Candle.

Accipe Lucernam ardentem in manibus tuis, de bonis operibus exempla demonstrans, Deoque perpetuo benedicens, qui fecit tecum misericordiam suam.

R.—Amen.

He then rises and kneeling down, intones the Hymn, Veni, Creator.

Hymnus.

Veni, Creator Spiritus,
    Mentes tuorum visita,
    Imple superna gratia,
    Quæ tu creasti pectora.

Qui diceris Paraclitus,
    Altissimi donum Dei,
    Fons vivus, ignis, charitas,
    Et spiritalis unctio.

Tu septiformis munere,
    Digitus Paternæ Dexteræ,
    Tu rite promissum Patris,
    Sermone ditans guttura.

Accende lumen sensibus,
　Infunde amorem cordibus,
　Infirma nostri corporis
　Virtute firmans perpeti.

Hostem repellas longius,
　Pacemque dones protinus:
　Ductore sic te prævio.
　Vitemus omne noxium.

Per te sciamus da Patrem,
　Noscamus atque Filium,
　Teque utriusque Spiritum
　Credamus omni tempore.

Deo Patri sit gloria
　Et Filio, qui a mortuis
　Surrexit ad Paraclito,
　In sæculorum sæcula.

R.—Amen.

P.—Emitte Spiritum tuum, et creabuntur.

R.—Et renovabis faciem terræ.

OREMUS.

Deus, qui corda fidelium Sancti Spiritus il-
lustratione docuisti, da nobis in eodem Spiritu

recta sapere, et de ejus semper consolatione gaudere. Per Christum Dominum nostrum.

R.—Amen.

The Hymn and Prayer being finished, the newly-clothed Sister puts down the Candle, and the Corrector seating himself, will then address a short sermon to her, and if she wishes will change her name.

At the end of the discourse, the Corrector rises, and laying his hand on the head of the newly-clothed Sister, says :—

Dominus, qui incœpit in te opus bonum, ipse perficiat ad augendam in te suæ largitatis gratiam, et ad honorem Beatæ Mariæ Virginis, cujus mœroris habitum geris, et ego, auctoritate Reverendissimi Patris Prioris Generalis Servorum S. Mariæ, nec non Apostolico in hac parte Indulto : te carissimam Sororem N. in nomine Domini suscipio, et accepto, atque omnium bonorum, quæ per totum hunc Ordinem nostrum fient imposterum, participem te constituo. In nomine Dei Patris omnipotentis, qui per æterna sæcula vivit, et regnat.

R.—Amen.

RITE FOR RECEIVING AND CLOTHING THE ORDINARY TERTIARIES.

All being arranged as at page 116, *the Corrector, or his Deputy, kneeling before the Altar, the Brothers or Sisters present, and those about to be received, placed between two Brothers or Sisters, being on their knees, he will say :—*

P.—Adjutorium nostrum in nomine Domini.

R.—Qui fecit cœlum et terram.

P.—Ostende nobis Domine misericordiam tuam.

R.—Et salutare tuum da nobis.

- P.—Domine exaudi orationem meam.

R.—Et clamor meus ad te veniat.

Then rising, he says :—

P.—Dominus vobiscum.

R.—Et cum spiritu tuo.

OREMUS.

Actiones nostras, quæsumus Domine, aspirando præveni et adjuvando prosequere, ut cuncta nostra oratio et operatio, a te semper incipiat et per te cœpta finiatur. Per Christum Dominum nostrum.

R.—Amen.

Then after he has seated himself, the Brother or Sister to be received will say the Confiteor, *at the end of which, the Priest standing up, says* Misereatur, *etc.,* Indulgentiam, *etc., and then sprinkling him (or her) with holy water, says :—*

Lavare, carissime Frater (aut Soror) et mundus (*vel* munda) esto, aufer malam cogitationem ab oculis tuis, luctum Unigeniti fac tibi planctum amarum; educ quasi torrentem lacrymas, ut benedictionem recipias a Domino, et misericordiam a Deo salutari suo.

R.—Amen.

He then blesses the Habit, saying :—

P.—Adjutorium nostrum in nomine Domini

R.—Qui fecit coelum et terram.

P.—Dominus vobiscum.

R.—Et cum spiritu tuo.

Blessing of the Scapular.

Oremus.

Domine Jesu Christe Rex Gloriæ, Pater misericordiarum, et Deus totius consolationis, qui tegimen nostræ mortalitatis induere dignatus es, obsecramus immensæ largitatis tuæ abundantiam, ut meritis B. M. semper Virginis, Septem BB. PP. Nostrorum, B. Philippi, et omnium Sanctorum bene✠dicere et sancti ✠ ficare digneris hoc genus vesti-

mentorum, quod Virgo Maria, Sanctique nostri
Patres ferre sanxerunt ad memoriam Dolorum,
quos ipsa B. Virgo sustinuit in Vita et Morte
Unigeniti Filii sui D. N. Jesu Christi, ut qui
eis usus fuerit, careat omni immunditia, libe-
retur a noxa; non secum resideat spiritus
superbiæ pæstilens, non cupiditas avaritiæ cor-
rumpens, non carnis vermis omnia inficiens,
sed te solum induere, et omni tua benedictione
cœlesti repleri mereatur. Per Christum Dominum nostrum.

R.—Amen.

THE GIRDLE.

OREMUS.

Omnipotens sempiterne Deus, qui pietatis
tuæ misericordiam quærentibus veniam peccatorum tribuisti, oramus immensam clementiam tuam, ut hanc Corrigiam bene ✠ dicere
et sancti ✠ ficare digneris, ut quicumque

D

lumbos suos ad evitandam concupiscentiam ex ea præcincti fuerint, continentiam perpetuam et misericordiam consequantur. Per Christum, etc.

R.—Amen.

If it be a Sister who is to be received, the following blessing of the Veil is added :—

OREMUS.

Quæsumus Omnipotens Deus, ut Velamina ista famulæ tuæ capiti suo imponenda bene ✠ dicere digneris, quatenus in ea ros tuæ benignitatis descendat, ut sint hæc Velamina in ejus cervicibus, honestas, humilitas, et sanitas cum omni benedictione Dei Patris et Filii et Spiritus Sancti per merita Beatissimæ semper Virginis Mariæ.

R.—Amen.

———

THE ROSARY AND BOOK.

OREMUS.

Domine Jesu Christe, Fili Dei vivi, qui

Discipulos tuos orare docuisti, suscipe, quæsumus, orationes famuli tui (*vel* famulæ tuæ, *aut* famulorum, *vel* famularum tuarum) quæ cum tua benedictione semper incipiant et per te cœptæ finiantur. Qui vivis et regnas, etc.

He then sprinkles all the Clothing with Holy Water.

Then kneeling on the steps in the middle of the Altar he intones the Hymn, Veni, Creator, *as at page* 123, *and it is sung alternately, all standing, except the Brother or Sister to be received. At the conclusion of the Hymn the Priest says :—*

P.—Emitte Spiritum tuum et creabuntur.

R.—Et renovabis faciem terræ.

P.—Domine exaudi orationem meam.

R.—Et clamor meus ad te veniat.

P.—Dominus vobiscum.

R.—Et cum spiritu tuo.

Oremus.

Omnipotens æterne Deus, propitiare peccatis

et ab omni servitute sæcularis habitus hunc famulum tuum (*vel* hanc famulam tuam) emunda, ut dum pomposa indumenta tuo amore deponit, tua gratia perfruatur, et hæreditatem consequi mereatur æternam. Per Christum Dominum nostrum.

R.—Amen.

The Priest then seats himself, and the Brother or Sister about to be received rises and kneels on the highest step of the Altar before him, all the others standing. Then the Priest, assisted by the Brothers or Sisters, divests him (or her) of the worldly dress, saying at the same time :—

Exuat te Deus, carissime Frater (*vel* carissima Soror) veterem hominem cum actibus suis, ut renoveris spiritu mentis tuæ, et induaris novum hominem qui secundum Deum creatus est in justitia et sanctitate in Christo Jesu Domino nostro.

R.—Amen.

This done, the Priest stands up and says:

Oremus.

Adesto Domine supplicationibus nostris et hunc famulum tuum (*vel* famulam tuam) bene ✠ dicere digneris, cui in Sancto Nomine tuo habitum Sacræ Religionis imponimus, ut te largiente, devotus (*vel* devota) in hac Sacra Religione persistere, et vitam percipere mereatur æternam. Per Christum Dominum nostrum.

R.—Amen.

He then again seats himself and clothes the Brother or Sister, saying :—

On giving the Scapular.

Accipe habitum munditiæ et humilitatis ut ita indutus (*vel* induta) observes ea, quæ regularibus institutis et majorum præceptis mandantur.

R.—Amen.

THE GIRDLE.

Accipe Corrigiam super lumbos tuos, ut sint præcincti in signum castitatis et temperantiæ.

R.—Amen.

If it be a Sister who is to be received, he then gives the Veil, saying:—

Accipe velamina candida cœlesti benedictione respersa in signum innocentiæ ad operiendum umbratilem capitis, pectorisque tui honestatem, atque ad æterni decoris speciem jucundissimam consequendam.

R.—Amen.

THE ROSARY AND BOOK.

Accipe signum Orationis in manibus tuis, ut more contemplantium præsentem vitam in patientia degas; atque futuram gloriam quærens, spreto mundo, cupias dissolvi et esse cum Christo.

R.—Amen.

On Giving the Lighted Candle.

Accipe Lucernam ardentem in manibus tuis, de bonis operibus exempla demonstrans, Deoque perpetuo benedicens, qui fecit tecum misericordiam suam.

R.—Amen.

The Novice then hands the Candle to another, himself (or herself) still kneeling. The Priest may then deliver a short discourse, and if it has been desired, may give the Novice a Religious name. He then stands up and says:—

P.—Ostende nobis Domine misericordiam tuam.

R.—Et salutare tuum da nobis.

P.—Domine exaudi orationem meam.

R.—Et clamor meus ad te veniat.

P.—Dominus vobiscum.

R.—Et cum spiritu tuo.

Oremus.

Deus, cui proprium est misereri semper et parcere, visita, quæso, hanc novam creaturam

tuam et meritis B. M. semper Virginis, sub
cujus triumphalis Passionis Vexillo in hac
nostra Religione Tibi militare exorsa est,
omnes insidias inimici tui ab ea longe repelle,
et Angeli tui Sancti habitent cum ea et in tua
pace custodiant, atque bene ✠ dictio tua sit
super eam semper. Per Christum Dominum
nostrum.

R.—Amen.

*Then holding his right hand over the head of
the Brother or Sister who has been received,
he says :—*

Dominus, qui incœpit in te, etc., *as at
page* 125.

RITE FOR THE PROFESSION OF THE
TERTIARIES.

*At the end of the year of the noviciate, (or
even before, if the Corrector shall deem fitting)*

*the profession will be proceeded with. Every-
thing therefore being prepared as above, at p.
116, the Brother or Sister Novice will approach
accompanied by two Brothers or Sisters respectively, and kneel with the same in the
middle of the Sanctuary, whereupon the Priest
standing up, will say :*

P.—Adjutorium nostrum in nomine Domini.

R.—Qui fecit cœlum et terram.

P.—Dominus vobiscum.

R.—Et cum spiritu tuo.

OREMUS.

Domine Jesu Christe, dux, salus, et forti-
tudo nostra, humiliter petimus, ut famulum
tuum (*vel* famulam tuam), quem (*vel* quam)
sanctæ compunctionis ardore, ab hujus sæculi
vanitate separasti, etiam a conversatione ter-
rena discernas, et gratiam, qua in te perse-
veret, infundas, ut protectionis tuæ præsidio
munitus (*vel* munita), quod, te donante, affec-

tat, te adjutore compleat. Qui vivis, et regnas in sæcula sæculorum. R.—Amen.

He then seats himself once more, and the Novice, with the companions, advances to the feet of the Priest, kneels down alone, and with his (or her) own lips, or if the Novice cannot read (by the lips of another) makes profession in the following form :—

"To the honour and glory of the Most Holy Trinity, the Father, the Son, and the Holy Ghost, of the Most Blessed Mary ever Virgin, of the Seven Blessed Founders, of St. Philip Benizi, and of all the Saints in Paradise, I, Brother (or Sister) N, in presence of you, Very Reverend Father, in the name of the the Most Reverend, the Father General of the Order of the Servants of the Blessed Virgin, promise for the future to live according to the Rule of the Tertiary Brothers (or Sisters) of the said Order, and this from henceforth until my death."

In the case where a vow of chastity is to be made, after the words, according to the Rule of the said Order, *is added*, "and to observe the Vow of Chastity."

After this the Priest stands up, and turning to the Altar, says :—

P —Sit nomen Domini benedictum.

R.—Ex hoc nunc, et usque in sæculum.

P.—Dominus vobiscum.

R.—Et cum spiritu tuo.

OREMUS.

Respice quæsumus Domine, super hunc, famulum tuum (*vel* hanc famulam tuam) N., qui (*vel* quæ) hodie pro tui nominis honore sæculo, et omnibus pompis, et vanitatibus ejus per nostræ servitutis ministerium voto. renunciavit, et eum (*vel* eam) Spiritus Sancti gratia perfunde, ut a peccatis omnibus absolutus (*vel* absoluta), et in ea confirmatus (*vel* confirmata), promissa semper impleat, et ad vitam æternam perveniat. Per Christum Dominum nostrum.

R.—Amen.

He then intones the Te Deum as at page
110, and at the end, says:—

P.—Confirma hoc Deus, quod operatus es
in nobis.

R.—A templo sancto tuo, quod est in
Jerusalem.

P.—Domine exaudi orationem meam.

R.—Et clamor meus ad te veniat.

P.—Dominus vobiscum.

R.—Et cum spiritu tuo.

OREMUS.

Sancte Spiritus, qui te Deum ac Dominum
mortalibus revelare dignatus es, immensam
tuam pietatis abundantiam suppliciter exor-
amus, ut sicut ubi vis, spiras, sic et huic
famulo tuo Fratri nostro (*vel* famulæ tuæ
Sorori nostræ) N. affectum piæ devotionis
inspires, et qui (*vel* quæ) tua sapientia est

conditus (*vel* condita), tua quoque providentia gubernetur : quem (*vel* quam) etiam unctio tua de omnibus doceat, et fac eum (*vel* eam) a sæculi vanitate ita veraciter converti, ut, quod hodie, te inspirante, inchoat, sic juste, pie, ac sancte per veram humilitatem, ac obedientiam, fraterna charitate fundatus (*vel* fundata), te adjuvante perficiat, ut in sancto proposito jugiter perseverans, ad vitam perveniat sempiternam.

Concede nos, famulos tuos, quæsumus Domine Deus, perpetua mentis, et corporis sanitate gaudere, et gloriosa Beatæ Mariæ semper Virginis intercessione, a præsenti liberari tristitia, et æterna perfrui lætitia.

Deus, qui ad recolendam memoriam dolorum Sanctissimæ Genitricis per Septem Beatos Patres nova Servorum ejus Familia Ecclesiam tuam fœcundasti, concede propitius, ita nos eorum consociari fletibus, ut perfruamur et gaudiis.

Adesto Domine supplicationibus nostris, quas in Beati Patris nostri Philippi Confessoris tui commemoratione deferimus, ut, qui nostræ justitiæ fiduciam non habemus, ejus, qui tibi placuit, precibus adjuvemur. Per Christum Dominum nostrum.

R.—Amen.

At the end, if he think fit, he will make a short address, and then dismiss the assembly.

FORM FOR GIVING TERTIARIES THE PAPAL BENEDICTION.

The Papal Benediction, by concession of His Holiness Leo XIII., is given twice a year, according to the formula of Benedict XIV., but not on the same day nor in the same place in which it is given by the Bishop. And since according to the said formula the Benediction is invoked upon the people, it cannot be given separately to individual Tertiaries, but to the assembled Congregation, and must be given by whomsoever shall preside over it, since it is understood that on him alone is conferred the power of imparting the Benediction. The Director or other authorised Priest, in cotta and white stole, without the assistance of acolytes, goes to the Altar, and first of all reads, or causes to be read, the following Rescript :

MOST HOLY FATHER.

The Father General of the Order of the Servants of Mary, humbly prostrate at the feet of your Holiness, entreats that the Tertiaries of his Order may twice a year receive the Papal Benediction with the Plenary Indulgence thereto attached.

And, etc., etc.

Sanctissimus Dominus noster Leo Papa XIII., in Audientia habita die 16 Decembris 1882, ab infrascripto Secretario Sacræ Con-

gregationis Indulgentiis sacrisque Reliquiis
præpositæ, benigne annuit pro gratia in omnibus juxta preces. Præsenti in perpetuum
valituro absque ulla Brevis expeditione.
Contrariis quibuscumque non obstantibus.
Datum Romæ ex Secretaria ejusdem S. Congregationis die 16 Decembris 1882.

Al. Card. OREGLIA a S. Steph. Præfectus.

FRANCISCUS DELLA VOLPE,
Secretarius.

Idem Pontifex simili Rescripto sub datum
Romæ die 15 Decembris anni 1883, eamdem
gratiam confirmavit adjiciens conditionem
præter Confessionem et Communionem, ut
singuli Summi Pontificis nomine Benedictionem accepturi, juxta mentem ipsius pias ad
Deum preces effundant, ut supra dicitur in
Summario Indulgentiarum et Privilegiorum pro
Tertiariis nostris utriusque sexus, num. VIII.

Then kneeling down he says :—

P.—Adjutorium nostrum in nomine Domini.

R.—Qui fecit cœlum et terram.

P.—Salvum fac populum tuum, Domine.

R.—Et benedic hæreditati tuæ.

P.—Dominus vobiscum.

R.—Et cum spiritu tuo.

Then, standing up, he says the following Prayer :

Oremus.

Omnipotens et misericors Deus, da nobis auxilium de Sancto, et vota populi hujus in humilitate cordis veniam peccatorum poscentis, tuamque benedictionem præstolantis et gratiam, clementer exaudi : dexteram tuam super eum benignus extende, ac plenitudinem divinæ benedictionis effunde : qua bonis omnibus cumulatus, felicitatem et vitam consequatur æternam.   Per Christum Dominum nostrum.   R.—Amen.

Then, going to the Epistle side of the Altar, and standing up, with a single Sign of the Cross, he gives the Blessing, pronouncing aloud these words :—

Benedicat vos Omnipotens Deus, Pater, ✠ Filius, et Spiritus Sanctus.

R.—Amen.

FORMULA OF THE BENEDICTION WITH THE PLENARY INDULGENCE FOR THE TERTIARIES.

In addition to the Papal Benediction, other Benedictions are given to the Tertiaries of the Servants of Mary, on certain days of the year, in accordance with the Decree of the Holy Congregation of Indulgences of the 15 December, 1888, quoted at page 54, for which His Holiness Pope Leo XIII. by the Bull, Quo universi, *of the 7th July*, 1882, *prescribed the following formula :—*

Antiph. Intret oratio mea in conspectu tuo, Domine; inclina aurem tuam ad preces nostras; parce Domine, parce populo tuo quem redemisti sanguine tuo pretioso, ne in æternum irascaris nobis.

Kyrie eleison. Christe eleison. Kyrie eleison.

Pater noster, *secreto.*

P.—Et ne nos inducas in tentationem.

R.—Sed libera nos a malo.

P.—Salvos fac servos tuos.

R.—Deus meus, sperantes in te.

P.—Mitte eis, Domine, auxilium de Sancto.

R.—Et de Sion tuere eos.

P.—Esto eis Domine turris fortitudinis.

R.—A facie inimici.

P.—Nihil proficiat inimicus in nobis.

R.—Et filius iniquitatis non apponat nocere nobis.

P.—Domine exaudi orationem meam.

R.—Et clamor meus ad te veniat.

P.—Dominus vobiscum.

R.—Et cum spiritu tuo.

Oremus.

Deus, cui proprium est misereri semper et parcere: suscipe deprecationem nostram, ut nos, et omnes famulos tuos, quos delictorum catena constringit, miseratio tuæ pietatis clementer absolvat.

Exaudi, quæsumus Domine, supplicum preces, et confitentium tibi parce peccatis : ut pariter nobis indulgentiam tribuas benignus et pacem.

Ineffabilem nobis, Domine, misericordiam tuam clementer ostende : ut simul nos et a peccatis omnibus exuas, et a pœnis, quas pro his meremur, eripias.

Deus, qui culpa offenderis, pœnitentia placaris; preces populi tui supplicantis propitius respice; et flagella tuæ iracundiæ, quæ pro peccatis nostris meremur, averte. Per Christum Dominum nostrum.

R —Amen.

The General Confession is then made by the Tertiaries, as follows :

Confiteor Deo omnipotenti, Beatæ Mariæ semper Virgini, Beato Michaeli Archangelo, Beato Joanni Baptistæ, Sanctis Apostolis Petro et Paulo, septem Beatis Patribus nostris, omnibus Sanctis, et tibi Pater, quia peccavi nimis cogitatione, verbo et opere : mea culpa, mea culpa, mea maxima culpa. Ideo precor Beatam Mariam semper Virginem, Beatum Michaelem Archangelum, Beatum Joannem Baptistam, Sanctos Apostolos Petrum et Paulum, septem Beatos Patres nostros, omnes Sanctos, et te Pater, orare pro me ad Dominum Deum nostrum.

Then the Corrector says :

Misereatur vestri, etc.

Indulgentiam, etc.

Dominus noster Jesus Christus, qui Beato Petro Apostolo dedit potestatem ligandi atque solvendi, Ille vos absolvat ab omni vinculo delictorum, ut habeatis vitam æternam, et vivatis in sæcula sæculorum. Amen.

Per sacratissimam Passionem et Mortem Domini nostri Jesu Christi; precibus et meritis Beatissimæ semper Virginis Mariæ, Beatorum Apostolorum Petri et Pauli, septem Beatorum Patrum Nostrorum et omnium Sanctorum, auctoritate a Summis Pontificibus mihi concessa, plenariam Indulgentïam omnium peccatorum vestrorum vobis impertior. In nomine Patris, ✠ et Filii, et Spiritus Sancti. Amen.

If this Indulgence be imparted immediately after the sacramental absolution, the Priest omitting all the rest, begins directly at the words: Dominus nostei Jesus Christus, *etc., and then substitutes throughout the singular for the plural number. If circumstances do*

*not permit the use of the entire formula, the
Priest, omitting the rest may say :*

Auctoritate a summis Pontificibus mihi concessa, plenariam omnium peccatorum tuorum
Indulgentiam tibi impertior.　In nomine Patris, ✠ et Filii, et Spiritus Sancti.

R.—Amen.

ABSOLUTION AT THE HOUR OF DEATH.

*In imparting the Plenary Indulgence to the
Tertiaries in case of death, the Corrector, or
any approved Confessor, will use the formula
prescribed by Pope Benedict XIV. in the
terms of the above-named Bull,* Quo universi
*of His Holiness Pope Leo XIII.　Entering
the room of the sick person, he will say :—*

P.—Pax huic domui.

R.—Et omnibus habitantibus in ea.

He then sprinkles the sick person with Holy

Water, and also the room and those present, saying:—

Asperges me, Domine, hyssopo, et mundabor, lavabis me et super nivem dealbabor.

Miserere mei, Deus, secundum magnam misericordiam tuam.

P.—Gloria Patri, etc.

R.—Sicut erat, etc.

He then repeats the Antiphon, Asperges me, etc.

P.—Adjutorium nostrum in nomine Domini.

R.—Qui fecit cœlum et terram.

Ant. Ne reminiscaris, Domine, delicta famuli tui (*vel* ancillæ tuæ), neque vindictam sumas de peccatis ejus.

Kyrie eleison. Christe eleison. Kyrie eleison.

Pater noster, *secreto.*

P.—Et ne nos inducas in tentationem.

R.—Sed libera nos a malo.

P.—Salvum fac servum tuum (*vel* salvam fac ancillam tuam).

R.—Deus meus, sperantem in te.

P.—Domine exaudi orationem meam.

R.—Et clamor meus ad te veniat.

P.—Dominus vobiscum.

R.—Et cum spiritu tuo.

Oremus.

Clementissime Deus, Pater misericordiarum, et Deus totius consolationis, qui neminem vis perire in te credentem, atque sperantem : secundum multitudinem miserationum tuarum respice propitius famulum tuum· N. (*vel* ancillam tuam N.), quem (*vel* quam) Tibi vera Fides et Spes Christiana commendant. Visita eum (*vel* eam) in salutari tuo et per Unigeniti tui Passionem, et Mortem, omnium ei delictorum suorum remissionem, et veniam clementer indulge : ut ejus anima in hora exitus sui te Judicem propitiatum inveniat, et in Sanguine ejusdem Filii tui ab omni macula abluta,

transire ad vitam mereatur perpetuam. Per
eumdem Christum Dominum nostrum. Amen.

*Then, after one of the Assisting Clerks has
recited the* Confiteor, *adding after the names
of the Apostles, the words,* septem Beatis Patribus nostris, *and doing the same in the
second part of the Confiteor, the Priest says :*
Misereatur, Indulgentiam, etc. *And then
continues :*

Dominus noster Jesus Christus Filius Dei
vivi, qui Beato Petro Apostolo suo dedit potestatem ligandi atque solvendi, per suam
piissimam misericordiam recipiat confessionem
tuam, et restituat tibi stolam primam, quam
in Baptismate recepisti : et ego, facultate mihi
ab Apostolica Sede tributa, Indulgentiam
Plenariam, et remissionem omnium peccatorum tibi concedo. In nomine Patris, ✠ et
Filii, et Spiritus Sancti.

Per sacrosancta humanæ reparationis mys-
teria, remittat tibi omnipotens Deus, omnes

præsentis, et futuræ vitæ pœnas, Paradisi portas aperiat, et ad gaudia sempiterna perducat. Amen.

Benedicat te, omnipotens Deus, Pater, ✠ et Filius, et Spiritus Sanctus. Amen.

In case, however, the sick person is nigh unto death, so that there is not time to use either the General Confession or the Prayers, the Priest shall immediately impart the Indulgence to him, saying : Dominus noster, etc.

And if death be still more imminent, he shall say :

Indulgentiam plenariam et remissionem omnium peccatorum tibi concedo, in nomine Patris, ✠ et Filii, et Spiritus Sancti. Amen.

This same formula of Absolution in Articulo mortis, serves also for the members of the Confraternity of Our Lady of Seven Dolours.

PRAYERS FOR THE MONTHLY MEETINGS.

AT THE COMMENCEMENT OF THE MEETING.

Veni, Sancte Spiritus, reple tuorum corda fidelium, et tui amoris in eis ignem accende.

P.—Emitte Spiritum tuum et creabuntur.

R.—Et renovabis faciem terræ.

P.—Memento congregationis tuæ.

R.—Quam possedisti ab initio.

P.—Domine exaudi orationem meam.

R.—Et clamor meus ad te veniat.

P.—Dominus vobiscum.

R.—Et cum spiritu tuo.

OREMUS.

Mentes nostras, quæsumus Domine, lumine tuæ claritatis illustra, ut videre possimus quæ agenda sunt, et quæ recta sunt agere valeamus. Per Christum Dominum nostrum.

R.—Amen.

The Hail Mary *is then said.*

At the Close of the Meetings.

Agimus Tibi gratias, Omnipotens Deus, pro universis beneficiis tuis. Qui vivis et regnas in sæcula sæculorum. Amen.

P.—Oremus pro benefactoribus nostris.

R.—Retribuere dignare Domine, omnibus nobis bona facientibus, propter nomen tuum, vitam æternam. Amen.

Ant.—Si iniquitates.

De profundis clamavi ad te Domine : * Domine exaudi vocem meam.

Fiant aures tuæ intendentes : * in vocem deprecationis meæ.

Si iniquitates observaveris Domine : * Domine quis sustinebit ?

Quia apud te propitiatio est : * et propter legem tuam sustinui te Domine.

Sustinuit anima mea in verbo ejus : * speravit anima mea in Domino.

A custodia matutina, usque ad noctem : * speret Israel in Domino.

Quia apud Dominum misericordia : * et copiosa apud eum redemptio.

Et ipse redimet Israel : * ex omnibus iniquitatibus ejus.

Requiem æternam : * dona eis. Domine.

Et lux perpetua : * luceat eis.

· *Ant.*—Si iniquitates observaveris Domine, Domine quis sustinebit ?

Kyrie eleison.

Christe eleison.

Kyrie eleison.

Pater noster, *secreto.*

P.—Et ne nos inducas in tentationem.

R.—Sed libera nos a malo.

P.—A porta inferi.

R.—Erue Domine animas eorum.

P.—Requiescant in pace.

R.—Amen.

P.—Domine exaudi orationem meam.

R.—Et clamor meus ad te veniat.

P.—Dominus vobiscum.

R.—Et cum spiritu tuo.

OREMUS.

Absolve quæsumus, Domine, animas Fratrum nostrorum defunctorum ab omni vinculo delictorum, ut in resurrectionis gloria, inter sanctos, et electos tuos resuscitati respirent. Per Christum Dominum nostrum. Amen.

P.—Requiem æternam dona eis, Domine.

R.—Et lux perpetua luceat eis.

P.—Requiescant in pace.

R.—Amen.

The Corrector then gives the Benediction either with the Blessed Sacrament, or with the formula, Benedictio Dei Omnipotentis, Patris, ✠ et Filii, et Spiritus Sancti, descendat super vos, et maneat semper. Amen.

————

PRAYERS
FOR THE MEETINGS OF THE DISCREET OR COUNCILLORS.

AT THE COMMENCEMENT OF THE MEETING.

Veni, Sancte Spiritus, etc., *as at the Monthly Meetings at page* 156.

AT THE CLOSE OF THE MEETING.

Agimus Tibi gratias, omnipotens Deus, pro universis beneficiis tuis. Qui vivis, etc.

P.—Confirma hoc Deus, quod operatus es in nobis.

R.—A templo sancto tuo quod est in Jerusalem.

P.—Memento Congregationis tuæ.

R.—Quam possedisti ab initio.

P.—Domine exaudi orationem meam.

R.—Et clamor meus ad te veniat.

P.—Dominus vobiscum.

R.—Et cum spiritu tuo.

OREMUS.

Præsta nobis, quæsumus, Domine, auxiliúm gratiæ tuæ, ut quæ, te auctore, facienda cognovimus, te adjuvante implere valeamus.

Interveniat pro nobis, quæsumus Domine Jesu Christe, nunc et in hora mortis nostræ apud tuam clementiam Beata Virgo Maria Mater tua, cujus sacratissimam animam in hora tuæ passionis doloris gladius pertransivit. Per te Jesu Christe, Salvator mundi, qui cum Patre et Spiritu Sancto vivis et regnas in sæcula sæculorum. Amen.

Benedictio Dei Omnipotentis, Patris, ✠ et Filii, et Spiritus Sancti descendat super vos, et maneat semper. Amen.

METHOD TO BE FOLLOWED IN THE ELECTION OF THE OFFICIALS AND OF THE DISCREET.

All the electors being assembled in the place appointed for the elections, the Corrector will

E

intone on his knees the Veni, Creator Spiritus, *which he will sing alternately with the others. At the close, he will repeat the versicle and prayer as at page 124, and will recite the* Hail Mary. *He will then proceed to the elections which will be conducted as prescribed by the Directory at page 103.*

The elections completed, and the names of those elected having been announced, the Corrector will then intone the hymn Te Deum, *at the end of which he will recite the versicles and prayers and give the Benediction as at page 110.*

DAYS OF THE STATIONS OF ROME.

1st January.—Circumcision
of Our Lord...............
6th—Epiphany of Our Lord
Septuagesima Sunday.........
Sexagesima Sunday ....
Quinquagesima Sunday ......
} Indulgence of thirty years and thirty quarantines.

Ash Wednesday.—Indulgence of fifteen years and fifteen quarantines.

Thursday ....
Friday ....
Saturday ....
1st Sunday of Lent ....
Monday ....
Tuesday ....
Wednesday ....
Thursday ....
Friday ....
Saturday ....
2nd Sunday of Lent............
Monday ....
Tuesday ....
Wednesday ....
Thursday ....
Friday ....
Saturday ....
3rd Sunday in Lent............
Monday ....
} Indulgence of ten years and ten quarantines.

Tuesday.............	
Wednesday	Indulgence of
Thursday ....~...............	ten years and
Friday	ten quarantines.
Saturday	

4th Sunday in Lent. — Indulgence of fifteen
years and fifteen quarantines.

Monday	
Tuesday..........................	
Wednesday	
Thursday	
Friday	
Saturday	Indulgence of
Passion Sunday	ten years and ten
Monday	quarantines
Tuesday..........................	
Wednesday	
Thursday	
Friday	
Saturday	

Palm Sunday.—Indulgence of twenty-five years
and twenty-five quarantines.

Monday	Indulgence of
Tuesday......	ten years and ten
Wednesday in Holy Week ...	quarantines.

Holy Thursday, *after Confession & Communion*,
PLENARY INDULGENCE.

Good Friday...	Indulgence of
Holy Saturday	30 years and 30
	quarantines.

Easter Sunday, *after Confession & Communion*,
PLENARY INDULGENCE.

Monday............ ⎞
Tuesday............ ⎟
Wednesday ...... ⎟ In Easter
Thursday .... ⎟ Week.
Friday .... ⎟
Saturday .... ⎠
Low Sunday, ...
25 Ap., Fst. of St. Mark. Evan.
Monday............ ⎞ Rogation
Tuesday............ ⎟ Days.
Wednesday ...... ⎠

Indulgence of thirty years and thirty quarantines.

Ascension Day, *after Confession & Communion*,
PLENARY INDULGENCE.

Saturday, the Vigil of Pentecost—Indulgence of ten years and ten quarantines.

Whit-Sunday ....
Monday............................
Tuesday...........................
Wednesday ....
Thursday ....
Friday ....
Saturday ....

Indulgence of thirty years and thirty quarantines.

Wednesday, Friday, and Saturday of Ember-Week in September..............
1st Sunday of Advent ....
2nd Sunday of Advent ......

Indulgence of ten years and ten quarantines.

Third Sunday of Advent.—Indulgence of fifteen years and fifteen quarantines.

Wednesday, Friday, and Saturday of Ember-Week in December... ....
4th Sunday of Advent.........
} Indulgence of ten years and ten quarantines.

24 Dec.—Vigil of the Nativity
25 Dec.—Nativity of our Lord
At the first Mass at midnight
At the second Mass at break of day......................
} Indulgence of fifteen years and fifteen quarantines.

At the third Mass, and during the remainder of aforesaid day, *after Confession and Communion*, PLENARY INDULGENCE

On the Feasts of St. Stephen Protomartyr, of St. John, Ap. and Ev., and of the Holy Innocents.
} Indulgence of thirty years and thirty quarantines.

SUMMARY

OF THE

INDULGENCES OF THE CHURCHES OF THE ORDER.

PLENARY INDULGENCES.

I.—To all those who, being truly penitent, after Confession and Communion, shall visit a Church of the Order, from the First Vespers until sunset, on any of the Feasts of Our Lord, and on two of the seven Festivals of the Blessed Virgin, to be selected once and for all, by the local Superiors, and on the Feasts of the Seven Dolours, which is usually solemnized on the third Sunday of September (although the feast may be canonically transferred to some other day), provided they shall recite seven *Our Fathers* and seven *Hail Marys*, or the Vespers of the Dead, and shall pray for the exaltation of Our Holy Mother the Church, for the extirpation of heresies, for the conversion of heretics and infidels and for the well-being of the reigning Roman Pontiff; and with regard to the last of the said solemnities, provided they also pray before the Altar or in the Chapel of the Seven Dolours. (Clement XII. *Unigeniti Filii Dei*, 19th December, 1734).

These Indulgencies, all the above-mentioned conditions having been fulfilled, may be gained by the Faithful, who either visit any Church of the Order, or accompany the solemn Procession which takes place in all the Churches of the said Order, on the festivity above-named. (Benedict XIV. Decree of the Holy Congregation of Indulgences and Sacred Relics, 3rd August, 1748.)

The days on which the aforesaid Indulgencies may be gained, shall be for the future, in regard to the first, the solemnity of Easter, and in regard to all the others, the Feasts of

Assumption and of the Nativity of Our Lady.

II.—To all the Faithful of either sex, who, being truly contrite, and having confessed and communicated, shall offer for some space of time at the " Forty Hours' " continuous and uninterrupted Prayers, (to be held only once in the year by license of the Ordinary of the place, in anyone of the aforesaid Churches of the Order), and shall there pray to the Lord. (Clement XII., passage before cited.)

III.—Every year, to all the Faithful of either sex, who, being truly contrite, and having confessed and communicated, shall devoutly visit any one of the Churches of the Order, even of the Nuns belonging to the same, from the first Vespers until sunset, on any of the seven days preceding and following the Feast of our Blessed Lady of Seven Dolours, celebrated at different times according to the convenience of the place, and shall there offer to God devout prayers for the concord of Christian Princes, for the extirpation of heresies, and for the exaltation of our Holy Mother the Church, the Indulgence to be gained on any one of the aforesaid days, to be chosen at pleasure, on which the prescribed works are performed. (Benedict XIV. *In supremo*, 6th September, 1745.

IV.—To each and all of the Faithful of either sex, who being truly contrite, and having confessed and communicated, shall devoutly visit any Church of the Order on some Feast, or day of each year, to be appointed in the aforesaid several Churches by the respective Provincial Superior, and shall there devoutly pray according to the intentions of the Supreme Pontiff. (Benedict XIV. Decree of the Holy Congregation of Indulgences and Sacred Relics, 12th April, 1747.)

The day appointed for the visit to the Church for gaining the Indulgence, shall, in the future, be the Feast of Corpus Christi.

But in regard to the Papal Benediction the custom of each Convent may be retained.

V.—To each and all the Faithful of either sex, who, being truly penitent, and having confessed and communicated, on the Feast of St. Philip Benizi (which is celebrated on the 23rd of August), between the first Vespers and sunset, on the above-mentioned Feast, shall devoutly visit any Church of the Order, whether of Monks or Nuns, and shall there pray for the concord of Christian Princes, for the extirpation of heresies, and for the exaltation of our Holy Mother the Church. (Clement X. Bull *Redemptoris et Domini*, 4th July, 1673)

VI.—To each and all the Faithful of either sex, who, being truly contrite and having confessed and communicated, shall, on the Feast of St. Peregrine Laziosi, (the 30th day of April), devoutly visit, between the first Vespers and sunset, any Church of the Order, whether of Monks or Nuns, and shall there pray for the concord of Christian Princes, for the extirpation of heresies, and for the exaltation of Holy Mother Church. (Benedict XIII. Bull, *Redemptoris et Domini*, 30th September, 1727.)

VII.—To each and all the Faithful of either sex, who, being truly contrite, and having confessed and communicated, shall, on the Feast of St. Juliana Falconieri (the 19th day of June), devoutly visit, between the first Vespers and sunset, on the aforesaid Feast, any Church of the Order, whether of Monks or Nuns, and shall there pray to God for the concord of Christian Princes, for the extirpation of heresies, and for the exaltation of Holy Mother Church. (Clement XIII. *Redemptoris et Domini*, 3rd July, 1737.)

VIII.—To each and all the Faithful of either sex, who, being truly contrite, and having confessed and communicated, shall devoutly assist for some space of time at the Exposition of the Blessed Sacrament, solemnised in honour of the Seven Dolours of the Blessed Virgin Mary, and in memory of the Passion of Our Lord Jesus Christ, by permission of the Ordinary of each place, in all the Churches of the Friars-Servants of Mary, in whatsoever place they are found, on a Friday, or any other day of the week to be appointed once and for ever by the aforesaid respective Ordinaries, according to the convenience of the places, and shall there pray to God for the concord of Christian Princes, and for the exaltation of Holy Mother Church, is granted a Plenary Indulgence once a month only, on one of the Fridays or other days aforesaid, to be selected by each of the Faithful at his own discretion. (Clement XIII. *Ad augendam fidelium religionem*, 20th December, 1762.)

IX.—To all the Faithful of either sex, being truly contrite, and having confessed and communicated, shall on the Friday after Passion Sunday, devoutly visit one of the aforesaid Churches, and shall there, for some space of time pray as above. (Pius VI. Bull of the 8th July, 1785.)

X.—To all the Faithful of either sex, who, being truly contrite, and having confessed and communicated, shall on a day to be selected by the Ordinary of the place, devoutly visit one of the aforesaid Churches, and pray as above. (Pius VI., as above-cited.)

The day selected for gaining this Indulgence is the Feast of the Seven Blessed Founders of the Order.

XI.—To all the Faithful of either sex, who, being truly penitent, and having confessed and communicated, shall devoutly visit a Church of the Order, on the day to be selected by the Ordinary of the place, on which is celebrated the solemn Anniversary of the Deceased Brothers and Sisters of the Confraternity of the Seven Dolours of the Blessed Virgin Mary. (Pius VI., as above-cited.)

The anniversary of the Commemoration of the Brothers and Sisters Departed is, except in Bologna, the first week-day after the Commemoration of all the Faithful Departed. At Bologna it is the Octave of the Faithful Departed.

XII.—By all the Faithful of either sex, who, being truly penitent, and having confessed and communicated, a Plenary Indulgence may be gained on the first and last day of the Novena of the Nativity of Our Lord Jesus Christ, provided they devoutly assist at the said Novena in a Church of the Order. (Pius VI., as above-cited.)

PARTIAL INDULGENCES.

I.—An Indulgence of fifty days to all the Faithful who shall at least with devout contrition visit on some day of the year a Church of the Order, and shall there recite at least one *Our Father* and one *Hail Mary* for all the Faithful living, and in intercession for the Departed.   (Clement XII. Bull *Unigeniti Filii Dei*, 19 December, 1734.)

II.—Indulgence of a hundred days to whomsoever shall, in a Church of the Order, devoutly assist at the chanting or recitation of the Canonical Hours, or at the chanting or recitation of the antiphon *Salve Regina*, which is every day chanted or recited in the Churches of the said Order and shall there pray to God for the exaltation of Holy Mother Church, for the extirpation of heresies, for the conversion of infidels, for peace, concord, and union among Christian Princes, and for the well-being of the reigning Roman Pontiff.   (Clement XII. as above-cited.)

III.— An Indulgence, likewise, of a hundred days to whomsoever shall devoutly visit the

Churches of the Order, between the First Vespers and sunset on the anniversary of their dedication. (Clement XII. as above-cited.)

IV.—Indulgence of a hundred days to whomsoever, being truly contrite, and having devoutly confessed, shall visit the Churches of the Order on any Saturday and there pray as above. (Clement XII. as before cited.)

V.—Indulgence of seven years and seven quarantines, to be gained once on each of the days, by all those, who, being truly contrite, and having confessed and communicated, shall visit one of the Churches of the Order between Septuagesima Sunday and Palm Sunday inclusively, and on Wednesday, Thursday, and Friday in Holy Week, and shall there recite the *Our Father* and *Hail Mary* seven times. (Clement XII. as above-cited.)

VI.—An Indulgence, likewise, of seven years and seven quarantines to all the aforesaid, who, being truly contrite, and having confes-

sed and communicated, shall on the third
Friday of each month, (except those included
between Septuagesima and Palm Sunday),
visit the Churches of the Order, and shall
there devoutly recite seven *Our Fathers* and
seven *Hail Marys*, or the Vespers of the
Dead. (Clement XII. as above-cited.)

VII.—An Indulgence, likewise, of seven
years and seven quarantines, to whomsoever
shall visit a Church of the Order on the Feasts
of S. Joseph, S. Augustine, and of all the
Saints of the Order (13 November), provided
that they shall have performed the works prescribed above. (Clement XII., before cited.)

VIII.—Indulgence, likewise, of seven years
and seven quarantines to whomsoever shall
visit the Churches of the Order, between the
First Vespers and sunset on the days of the
Invention and Exaltation of the Holy Cross,
and on the several days of their respective
Octaves, provided they shall perform the

works above-prescribed, and give an alms. (Clement XII. as above-cited.)

IX.—An Indulgence, likewise, of seven years and seven quarantines, to all the foregoing, who, being truly contrite and having confessed and communicated, shall visit the Churches of the Order on all the other Feasts of Our Lord Jesus Christ, and on the other five Feasts of the Blessed Virgin, and on the eight days following the Feast of Our Blessed Lady of Dolours (usually celebrated on the third Sunday in September) though it may happen that the said Feast may be canonically transferred to another day. (Clement XII. as above-cited.)

X.—Indulgence of seven years and seven quarantines, to those who, being truly contrite and having confessed and communicated, shall devoutly assist for some time at the Exposition of the Blessed Sacrament, usually held in honour of the Seven Dolours of the Bles⌐

Virgin and in memory of the Passion of Our Lord Jesus Christ, by licence of the respective Ordinaries of the various places, in the Churches of the Friars of the Order of the Servants of Mary, in whatever place they may be, on a Friday or other day of every week to be appointed once for ever according to the exigences of the place; and shall there pray to God for the concord of Christian Princes, the extirpation of heresies, and the exaltation of Holy Mother Church. Which Indulgence may be gained every Friday or other day as above, except on the one (to be chosen at discretion by each of the Faithful), on which they shall have gained the Plenary Indulgence. (Pope Clement XIII. *Ad augendam fidelium religionem*, 20 *December*, 1762.)

XI. Indulgence of seven years and seven quarantines to be gained on every day of the Novena of the Nativity of Our Lord Jesus Christ, by those who, at least with true contrition shall devoutly assist at the prayers of the said Novena, in the Churches of the Order. (Pope Pius VI. Bull of 8 July, 1785.)

XII.—Indulgence of seven years and seven quarantines to all the Faithful each time that they shall devoutly assist at the public recitation of the Rosary of the Seven Dolours of the Blessed Virgin, which takes place in the Churches of the Order at the time of the first Mass.* (Gregory XVI. Rescript of the Holy Congregation of Indulgences, 11 July, 1831.)

The Holy Congregation of Indulgences has recognised as authentic the foregoing summary, and has graciously permitted it to be printed. From the Secretary's Office of the said Congregation, 12th January, 1884.

Louis Card. Oreglia di S. Stefano.
Prefect.

✠

FRANCIS DELLA VOLPE,
Secretary.

* In England the Rosary is said at Benediction. at which time the Faithful may gain the abov' mentioned Indulgences.

CALENDAR

Of the Saints and Blessed of the Order, and of the Days on which Indulgences may be gained.

JANUARY.

1. Blessed Bonfiglio Monaldi of Florence, the first of the Seven Blessed Founders. *Indulgence of the Stations of Rome.*

6. Epiphany of Our Lord. *Indulgence of the Stations of Rome.*

14. Anniversary of the death of the Parents of the Monks and Nuns of our Order.

17. Dedication of our Basilica of the SSma Annunziata in Florence,

FEBRUARY.

2. Purification of the B.V.M. *Plenary Indulgence for the Tertiaries.*

10. Vigil of the Seven Founders. *Fast for the Tertiaries.*

11. Solemnity of the Seven Blessed Founders of our Order. *Benediction with Plenary Indulgence for the Tertiaries.*

17. Blessed Alexis Falconieri of Florence, one of the Seven Blessed Founders.

19. Blessed Elizabeth Picenardi of Mantua, Virgin, of the Third Order.

Septuagesima Sunday... ⎫
Sexagesima   „   ... ⎬ Indulgences of the Stations of Rome.
Quinquagesima „   ... ⎭

Ash Wednesday, and every day in Lent up to Low Sunday. *Indulgences of the Stations of Rome.*

MARCH.

19. St. Joseph, Spouse of the Blessed Virgin. *Plenary Indulgence for the Tertiaries.*

25. Annunciation of the Blessed Virgin. *Plenary Indulgence for the Tertiaries.*

Friday in Passion Week. Commemoration of the Seven Dolours of our Lady. *Plenar⁷ Indulgence for the Tertiaries.*

APRIL.

9. Blessed Ubald Adimari, Florence, Conf.

16. Blessed Joachim Piccolomini, of Siena, Confessor.

18. Blessed Amadeus Amidei of Florence, one of the Seven Blessed Founders.

25. S. Mark, Ap. and Ev. *Indulgence of the Stations of Rome.*

30. St. Peregrine Laziosi, of Forli, Confessor. *Plenary Indulgence for the Tertiaries.*

Easter Sunday. *Benediction, with Plenary Indulgence for the Tertiaries.*

Second Sunday after Easter. Dedication of our Church of Monte Senario.   -

MAY.

3. Blessed Sostene Sostegni and Hugh Uguccioni of Florence, two of the Seven Blessed Founders.

28. Blessed James Philip Bertoni of Faenza, Confessor.

Rogation Days—Monday, Tuesday, and

Wednesday before Ascension Day. *Indulgences of the Stations of Rome.*

Ascension Day. *Indulgence of the Stations of Rome.*

Vigil of Pentecost. *Indulgence of the Stations of Rome.*

Whit-Sunday. *Benediction, with Plenary Indulgence for the Tertiaries, and Indulgence of the Stations of Rome every day up to the following Saturday.*

JUNE.

8.   Blessed Francis Patrizi of Siena, Conf.

18. Vigil of St. Juliana Falconieri. *Fast for the Tertiaries.*

19. St. Juliana Falconieri. Foundress of the Order of 'Mantellate.' *Benediction, with Plenary Indulgence for the Tertiaries.*

20. Blessed Benincasa of Florence, Confessor.

Corpus Christi. *Plenary Indulgence for the Tertiaries.*

JULY.

21. Blessed Thomas Corsini of Orvieto, Conf.

AUGUST.

15. Assumption of the Blessed Virgin. *Plenary Indulgence for the Tertiaries.*
20. Blessed Manetto dell' Antella of Florence, one of the Seven Blessed Founders.
23. Solemnity of our Holy Father, St. Philip Benizi of Florence, illustrious Propagator of the Order. *Benediction, with Plenary Indulgence for the Tertiaries.*
28. St. Augustine, Bishop and Doctor of the Church, and our Legislator.
31. Blessed Buonagiunta of Florence, one of Seven Blessed Founders of our Order.

SEPTEMBER.

1. Blessed Johanna Soderini of Florence, Virgin, of the Third Order.
3. Blessed Andrew Dotti of Borgo San Sepolcro, Confessor.

8. Nativity of the Blessed Virgin. *Plenary Indulgence of the Tertiaries.*

Saturday before the third Sunday. *Fast for the Tertiaries.*

Third Sunday. Solemnity of the Seven Dolours of the Blessed Virgin, Principal Foundress and Patroness of our Order. *Benediction, with Plenary Indulgence for the Tertiaries.*

Wednesday, Friday, and Saturday in Ember-Week. *Indulgence of the Stations of Rome.*

17. Anniversary of all the deceased Benefactors of the Order.

26. Translation of the Body of our Holy Father, St. Philip Benizi.

OCTOBER.

7. Blessed James, the Alms-giver, of Città-della Pieve. Confessor, of the Third Order.

Second Sunday, Dedication of all the Churches of the Order.

25. Blessed John Angelo Porro, of Milan, Confessor.

NOVEMBER.

The first Week-day after the Commemoration of the Faithful Departed, Anniversary of the Brothers and Sisters of the Confraternity clothed with the Habit.

Sunday within the octave of All Saints. Feast of the Saints whose Relics are venerated in the Churches of the Order.

13. Feast of all the Saints and Blessed of the Order.

14. Commemoration of all the Deceased Brothers of the Order.

DECEMBER.

1st, 2nd, 3rd, and 4th Sundays of Advent. *Indulgences of the Stations of Rome.*

8. Immaculate Conception of the Blessed Virgin. *Plenary Indulgence for the Tertiaries.*

12. Blessed Jerome Ranuzzi of S. Angelo in Vado, Confessor.

14. Blessed Bonaventure Bonaccorsi of Pistoia, Confessor.

Wednesday, Friday, and Saturday in Ember-Week. *Indulgences of the Stations of Rome.*

24. Vigil of the Nativity of Our Lord. *Indulgences of the Stations of Rome.*

25. Nativity of Our Lord. *At the first, second, and third Mass, Indulgence of the Stations of Rome. Benediction, with Plenary Indulgence for the Tertiaries.*

26. St. Stephen, Protomartyr. *Indulgences of the Stations of Rome.*

27. St. John the Evangelist. *Indulgences of the Stations of Rome.*

28. Holy Innocents. *Indulgences of the Stations of Rome.*

Twice a year, on days to be appointed by the Corrector, the Papal Benediction wit

Plenary Indulgence for the Tertiaries.

*Once a month, the day being at the choice
of each of the Tertiaries, on reciting five*
Our Fathers, *five* Hail Marys, *and five*
Glory be to the Fathers, *for the wants of
Holy Church, and one* Our Father, Hail
Mary, *and* Glory be to the Father, *for the
intentions of the Supreme Pontiff, the Indulgences of the Stations of Rome, of the Portiuncula, of the Holy Places of Jerusalem,
and of St. James of Compostella, may be
gained.*

———

NOTICE.

The S. Congregation of Indulgences concerning the question as to the day on which Indulgences may be gained when Feasts are transferred, has decreed that, in cases where a postponement of the "ceremonial" of a Feast takes place, the Indulgences shall be suspended until the keeping of the Feast; but that when only the Office and Mass, without the "exterior solemnity," are transferred, the Indulgences shall remain obtainable on the day originally fixed in the calendar. (Bull, *Urbis et Orbis*, 9 Aug., 1852.)

INDEX.

ERRATA.

Page 15, *read* Sixtus IV., *not* Sistus IV.

  ,, 17, ,,   Dum intra, *not* Dum inter.

  ,, 20, ,,   Lezana, *not* Legana.

  ,, 87, ,,   Who can read, will say, *not* Who can read the will.

  ,, 52, ,,   Enumerated, *not* Ennmerated.

  ,, 61, ,,   Notary, *not* Votary.

Ingram Content Group UK Ltd.
Milton Keynes UK
UKHW050640120323
418239UK00018B/590

9 780342 023783